Writing the Critical Essay

Obesity

An OPPOSING VIEWPOINTS® Guide

Lauri S. Friedman, *Book Editor*

OPPOSING
VIEWPOINTS®
SERIES

GREENHAVEN PRESS
A part of Gale, Cengage Learning

GALE
CENGAGE Learning™

Detroit • New York • San Francisco • New Haven, Conn • Waterville, Maine • London

GALE
CENGAGE Learning

Christine Nasso, *Publisher*
Elizabeth Des Chenes, *Managing Editor*

© 2009 Greenhaven Press, a part of Gale, Cengage Learning

LIBRARY OF CONGRESS CATALOGING-IN-PUBLICATION DATA

Obesity / Lauri S. Friedman, book editor.
    p. cm. — (Writing the critical essay: an opposing viewpoints guide)
  Includes bibliographical references and index.
  ISBN 978-0-7377-3463-8 (hardcover)
  1. Obesity. 2. Essay—Authorship. I. Friedman, Lauri S.
  RC628.O24 2008
  362.196'398—dc22
                                                              2008037875

Printed in the United States of America
1 2 3 4 5 6 7 12 11 10 09 08

CONTENTS

E xamining the state of writing and how it is taught in the United States was the official purpose of the National Commission on Writing in America's Schools and Colleges. The commission, made up of teachers, school administrators, business leaders, and college and university presidents, released its first report in 2003. "Despite the best efforts of many educators," commissioners argued, "writing has not received the full attention it deserves." Among the findings of the commission was that most fourth-grade students spent less than three hours a week writing, that three-quarters of high school seniors never receive a writing assignment in their history or social studies classes, and that more than 50 percent of first-year students in college have problems writing error-free papers. The commission called for a "cultural sea change" that would increase the emphasis on writing for both elementary and secondary schools. These conclusions have made some educators realize that writing must be emphasized in the curriculum. As colleges are demanding an ever-higher level of writing proficiency from incoming students, schools must respond by making students more competent writers. In response to these concerns, the SAT, an influential standardized test used for college admissions, required an essay for the first time in 2005.

Books in the Writing the Critical Essay: An Opposing Viewpoints Guide series use the patented Opposing Viewpoints format to help students learn to organize ideas and arguments and to write essays using common critical writing techniques. Each book in the series focuses on a particular type of essay writing—including expository, persuasive, descriptive, and narrative—that students learn while being taught both the five-paragraph essay as well as longer pieces of writing that have an opinionated focus. These guides include everything necessary to help students research, outline, draft, edit, and ultimately write successful essays across the curriculum, including essays for the SAT.

Using Opposing Viewpoints

This series is inspired by and builds upon Greenhaven Press's acclaimed Opposing Viewpoints series. As in the parent series, each book in the Writing the Critical Essay series focuses on a timely and controversial social issue that provides lots of opportunities for creating thought-provoking essays. The first section of each volume begins with a brief introductory essay that provides context for the opposing viewpoints that follow. These articles are chosen for their accessibility and clearly stated views. The thesis of each article is made explicit in the article's title and is accentuated by its pairing with an opposing or alternative view. These essays are both models of persuasive writing techniques and valuable research material that students can mine to write their own informed essays. Guided reading and discussion questions help lead students to key ideas and writing techniques presented in the selections.

The second section of each book begins with a preface discussing the format of the essays and examining characteristics of the featured essay type. Model five-paragraph and longer essays then demonstrate that essay type. The essays are annotated so that key writing elements and techniques are pointed out to the student. Sequential, step-by-step exercises help students construct and refine thesis statements; organize material into outlines; analyze and try out writing techniques; write transitions, introductions, and conclusions; and incorporate quotations and other researched material. Ultimately, students construct their own compositions using the designated essay type.

The third section of each volume provides additional research material and writing prompts to help the student. Additional facts about the topic of the book serve as a convenient source of supporting material for essays. Other features help students go beyond the book for their research. Like other Greenhaven Press books, each book in the Writing the Critical Essay series includes bibliographic listings of relevant periodical articles, books, Web sites, and organizations to contact.

Writing the Critical Essay: An Opposing Viewpoints Guide will help students master essay techniques that can be used in any discipline.

The Paradox of Obesity and Hunger in America

When people consider the problem of obesity, rarely do they factor hunger into the equation. On the surface, the problems of obesity and hunger seem like polar opposites: One is typically the result of too much food, the other, the result of too little. Yet both obesity and hunger are increasingly growing public health problems that are revealing themselves to be intrinsically connected, so much so that they often plague the same families and even the same individuals. Researchers are beginning to explore the link between these two seemingly contradictory problems in greater depth, and what they are finding is fascinating.

Hunger, or what is more broadly known as "food insecurity," contributes to obesity in several different ways. One is that low-income families have increasingly fewer dollars to spend on nutritious food. Indeed, when the price of basic commodities, including food, rose sharply in 2008, thousands of American families had to cut back on or change the type of groceries they bought. With fewer food dollars to spend, researchers explain that families have been forced to pick cheaper, high-calorie foods that fill them up temporarily but do not offer them proper nutrition, such as large-quantity fast food or dense, starchy foods like pasta. According to a jointly published report by the Center on Hunger and Poverty and the Food Research and Action Center (FRAC), "While families may get enough food to avoid feeling hungry, they also may be poorly nourished because they cannot afford a consistently adequate diet that promotes health and averts obesity. In the short term, the stomach registers that it is full, not whether a meal was nutritious."[1]

Another explanation for the "hunger-obesity paradox" is that food-insecure people tend to overeat when food is available. Studies of eating habits have revealed that when food is inconsistently available, people eat more than they normally would if it were plentiful. Over time, this type of stop-and-start "roller coaster" eating results in weight gain. The body, not knowing when its next meal will come, tends to reserve calories and lower metabolism in an effort to keep itself going for longer amounts of time. This is exactly why most nutritionists and doctors recommend eating five or six small meals each day to offer the body a steady stream of predictable caloric intake: to avoid the weight gain that is often accompanied by erratic eating.

Yet another factor tying together hunger and obesity is the lack of nutritious foods available in most low-income neighborhoods. High-quality cuts of meat, fish, fresh fruits, vegetables, and whole grains are often scarce in such places, due to the higher cost of producing, shipping, and storing them. Instead, stores in these areas are typically stocked with high-fat, high-sodium canned and processed foods that are cheaper yet less nutritious. According to a study of such neighborhoods in Los Angeles, "This lack of access to a variety of healthy foods limits the ability to make healthy choices"[2] and is a major factor in the hunger-obesity paradox.

These are just a few of the explanations offered by experts who have found evidence for the link between hunger and obesity. The data show the link is strong: A 2004 study of food insecurity and obesity among California residents, for example, found that 27 percent of all food-insecure residents were obese, and 36 percent were overweight. In fact, just 2 percent of all food-insecure or hungry California residents were underweight. The California study is just one resource demonstrating the increasingly clear link between being food insecure and overweight. This phenomenon has been found outside the United States, too: Data from South Africa, Iran, and other nations have confirmed a link between food-insecure families and obesity or overweight.

Women have been hit particularly hard by the hunger-obesity paradox. A 2001 study published in the *Journal of Nutrition* found that food-insecure women were 30 percent more likely to be overweight than women who were food secure. The authors of the study concluded that "although individuals with poor food security might be expected to have reduced food intake . . . food insecurity had an unexpected and paradoxical association with overweight status among women."[3] One explanation could be that low-income mothers often sacrifice their

Obesity in American children can be fought by providing them with healthy snacks such as fruits and vegetables.

New, creative ways to exercise, such as the video game Dance Dance Revolution, can help fight obesity by making exercise fun and enjoyable.

own nutritional needs for the sake of their children's. They are thus even more prone to the health risks of "roller coaster" eating and often save the most nutritious food available for their children.

According to a study conducted jointly by the Census Bureau and the U.S. Department of Agriculture, 30 million Americans qualify as hungry or food insecure each year. That number is expected to rise as a result of a worsening economy and higher food prices, and even more people are expected to begin relying on food banks and soup kitchens to get their next meal. At the same time, the American obesity epidemic showed no signs of slowing down. As public policy officials seek answers to these related problems, they will undoubtedly need to tackle the hunger-obesity paradox to get solutions to both problems. The link between hunger and obesity is just one of the topics explored in *Writing the Critical*

Essay: An Opposing Viewpoints Guide: Obesity. The causes of obesity, its related health risks, and to what extent the government is responsible for tackling the problem is explored in passionately argued viewpoints and model essays. Thought-provoking writing exercises help readers write their own persuasive essays on this compelling and timely subject.

Notes

1. Center on Hunger and Poverty and the Food Research and Action Center (FRAC), "The Paradox of Hunger and Obesity," July 17, 2003. www.centeronhunger.org/pdf/hungerandobesity.pdf.

2. County of Los Angeles Department of Health Services, "Food Insecurity," March 2004. http://lapublichealth.org/wwwfiles/ph/hae/ha/lahealthfoodinsec_0304.pdf.

3. Marilyn S. Townsend, Janet Peerson, Bradley Love, Cheryl Achterberg, and Suzanne P. Murphy, "Food Insecurity Is Positively Related to Overweight in Women," *Journal of Nutrition*, vol. 131, no. 6, 2001, p. 1738.

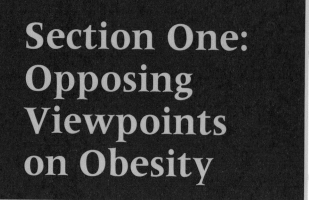

Section One:
Opposing
Viewpoints
on Obesity

The Problem of Obesity Is a Crisis

Dustin Wright and Eric Wright, Center for Urban Policy and the Environment

In the following essay the Center for Urban Policy and the Environment argues that obesity is a growing crisis in America, one that costs citizens, employers, health-care companies, and the government millions of dollars each year. The author explains that about 97 million American adults can be classified as obese—this amounts to nearly 30 percent of the entire population. Obesity is associated with diseases such as diabetes, heart disease, stroke, and cancer, which together kill hundreds of thousands of Americans each year. Given this, the author suggests that obesity should be classified as a disease in itself so insurance companies can help pay for treatment and prevention programs. Finally, the author concludes that the government should spearhead obesity-reduction programs in workplaces, schools, and communities in order to safeguard the health of its citizens.

The Center for Urban Policy and the Environment is a research organization in the School of Public and Environmental Affairs at Indiana University–Purdue University Indianapolis (IUPUI). Faculty and staff with expertise in program evaluation, policy analysis, facilitation, and planning work on a wide variety of policy issues, including obesity.

Dustin Wright and Eric Wright, Center for Urban Policy and the Environment, "Obesity Epidemic Burdens Healthcare System," healthpolicy.iupui.edu, October 2006. Reproduced by permission.

Consider the following questions:

1. How many Americans die from obesity-related causes each year, as reported by the author?
2. How many more days of work do obese male and female employees miss than employees of normal weight, according to the author?
3. What phrase was removed from the Centers for Medicare and Medicaid Services regulations in July 2004?

An estimated 97 million adults in the United States are obese or overweight, a number that has doubled in the last 30 years and is likely to continue to rise. The dramatic increase in the prevalence of overweight in our nation corresponds to an increase in related chronic diseases such as hypertension, high cholesterol, type 2 diabetes mellitus, heart disease, stroke, gallbladder disease, musculoskeletal disorders, and certain cancers. Each year, an estimated 300,000 adults in the United States die of causes associated with obesity. . . .

The Costs of Obesity

The costs of treating overweight and obese Americans have increased dramatically over time, and will continue to rise as the number of overweight and obese individuals in our society continues to increase. According to the National Health Accounts study (which includes institutionalized populations), nearly $79 billion was spent on medical expenses related to obesity in the United States in 1998. Nearly half of these costs were paid by Medicare and Medicaid. In addition, the mean number of primary care, specialty care, and diagnostic service visits in a one-year period—and the charges for these services—was significantly higher for obese patients than for similar patients of normal weight. Finally, the annual indirect costs of obesity-related diseases, such as lost wages and future earnings lost by premature death have been estimated at $47.6 billion.

The Impact of Obesity on Employers

Obesity also has a significant cost for employers throughout the United States, reflected in higher health insurance and workers compensation costs, as well as costs associated with absenteeism. The annual cost of obesity resulting from increased medical expenditures and absenteeism for a business with 1,000 employees has been estimated to be nearly $285,000 per year. In addition, the average annual per capita increase in medical expenditures and absenteeism associated with obesity has been reported to range from $460 to $2,500 per obese employee, a range that is positively correlated with the employee's BMI [body mass index]. The per capita cost is significantly higher

Due to unhealthy eating habits, obesity among Americans has doubled in the last 30 years and has led to an increase in related diseases such as diabetes and heart disease.

among women, with an increase of $1,370 to $2,485 per year. Also obese male employees miss an average of two more days of work each year than male employees of normal weight, and obese female employees miss five more work days than their normal weight counterparts. . . .

We Must Treat Obesity as a Disease

Given the high costs of healthcare, it is important to develop strategies for reducing the costs of obesity-related chronic diseases. One strategy is to treat obesity itself as a disease, and thus promote the acceptance of obesity treatment by private insurance companies, HMOs, Medicare, and Medicaid.

Currently, only *obesity-related diseases* (i.e, diabetes, hypertension, hypercholesterolemia, etc.) are routinely treated and reimbursed. However, some major organizations have begun to change their approach. For example, the World Health Organization and the Centers for Disease Control recently began classifying obesity as a distinct disease, and in 2002, the Internal Revenue Service officially recognized obesity as a disease and allowed expenses for obesity treatment to be claimed as a medical tax deduction. Furthermore, in July 2001, the U.S. Department of Health and Human Services and the Centers for Medicare and Medicaid Services (CMS) jointly announced that the specific phrase "Obesity itself cannot be considered an illness" had been removed from CMS regulations.

The Problem of Obesity Is a Crisis

As the world's wealthiest nation, the United States is also building the biggest bodies. It's hardly cause for patriotic pride.

Craig Lambert, "The Way We Eat Now: Ancient Bodies Collide with Modern Technology to Produce a Flabby, Disease-Ridden Populace," *Harvard Magazine*, May/June 2004, p. 50.

Insurance Companies Do Not Cover Obesity as a Disease

Despite the potential cost savings from improved approaches for obesity treatment, insurance companies are generally reluctant to cover preventive treatment.

Obesity Trends Among U.S. Adults

As a nation, Americans have gotten fatter. They have increased their body mass index (BMI), the measurement the government uses to determine whether a person is overweight or obese. A person is considered obese if his or her BMI is greater than 30, which is the equivalent, for a 5' 4" person, of being 30 pounds overweight.

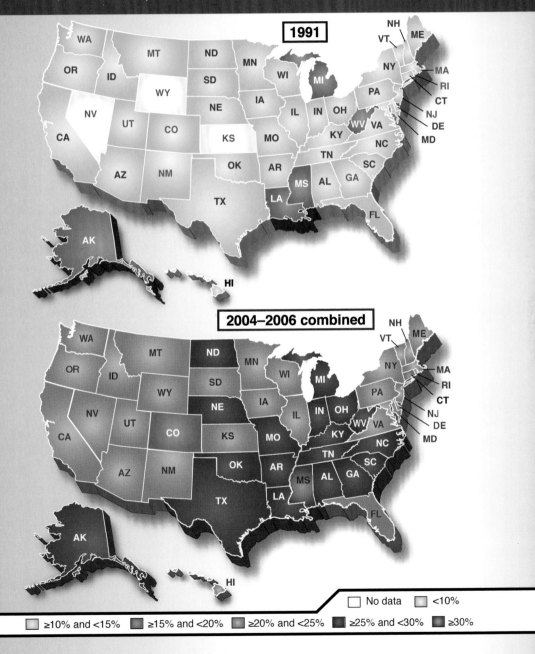

1991

2004–2006 combined

No data ☐ <10% ☐ ≥10% and <15% ☐ ≥15% and <20% ☐ ≥20% and <25% ☐ ≥25% and <30% ☐ ≥30%

Taken from: Behavioral Risk Factor Surveillance System, CDC.

Frequently, insurance companies indicate that they perceive low demand for expanded obesity management and they doubt that patients are willing to pay extra for it. If they are correct and there is a lack of demand for obesity management, it may be due in part to the overabundance of commercial weight-loss products and services for consumers (e.g., Weight Watchers, the Atkins Diet, etc.), an industry on which Americans spent an estimated $30 billion in 2000. Unfortunately, many of these products are not based on credible scientific evidence and are often unsuccessful at helping individuals achieve long-term weight management.

Insurance companies also rarely pay for medications to promote weight loss; 29 states specifically exclude these drugs from Medicaid reimbursement, as do more than 80 percent of employers who provide healthcare insurance to their employees. In fact, the Social Security Act mandates that a state that includes drugs for its Medicaid recipients must include all FDA-approved drugs *"except those used in the treatment of weight loss or weight gain."* Given that the costs savings obtained by treating obesity as a disease would not be immediate, insurers will likely need more empirical evidence of improved health outcomes or significant cost savings.

A Renewed Focus on Treatment and Prevention

Other ways to reduce healthcare costs related to overweight and its co-morbidities include public initiatives focusing on obesity treatment and prevention. These programs and initiatives should focus on supporting healthy school environments by increasing access to foods and beverages with higher nutritional quality, increasing health education requirements, and increasing opportunities for children to participate in physical activities. States can also support the planning and design of healthy communities through support for local efforts to make towns and cities more conducive to walking. In the workplace,

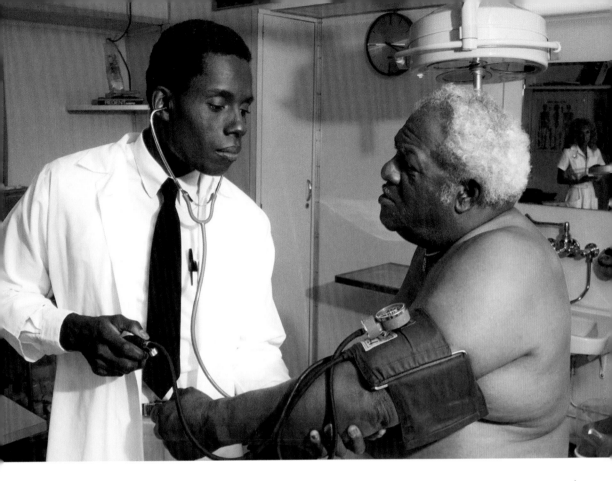

employers can support and sponsor programs that promote healthy eating habits and increase employee access to physical activities.

For the past few years, the federal government has provided funding to states for programs that address poor nutrition and inadequate physical activity. The Nutrition and Physical Activity Program to Prevent Obesity and Other Chronic Diseases helps states develop and implement science-based nutrition and physical activity interventions. The program's major goals are to balance caloric intake and expenditures; increase physical activity; improve nutrition through increased consumption of fruits and vegetables; reduce television time; and increase breastfeeding.

In 2005–2006 thus far, 21 states have each received $100,000 to $450,000 in funding for capacity building (i.e., data collection, building partnerships, and creating

Insurance companies have been reluctant to cover preventive treatment for obesity because of extra health-care costs.

statewide health plans), and 7 additional states have each received $750,000 to $1.3 million in funding for basic implementation (i.e., development of new interventions, evaluation of existing interventions, and support for additional state and local efforts to prevent obesity and other chronic diseases). . . .

Fighting the Obesity Problem

A number of programs, initiatives, and philosophical shifts show promise for reducing obesity rates and its associated costs. More overweight and obese individuals may become eligible for medical treatment of obesity as a disease as increasing numbers of healthcare professionals and insurance agencies change their perceptions of this problem. The increased access to obesity prevention and treatment services could reduce the number of obesity-related illnesses and diseases for millions of Americans each year, thus saving millions of dollars in annual healthcare expenditures. . . . The development of several public health initiatives holds some promise for helping to reduce the percentage of overweight and obese residents—a reduction that could eventually reduce associated healthcare expenditures. However, more work is needed, and the state could benefit from additional initiatives, legislation, funding, and programs that focus on lowering the average Body Mass Index of [Americans]. For example, obesity-reduction programs are most effective when they are integrated into the workplace; so employers should be more active in promoting obesity-risk screenings and fitness activities. In addition, employers should be made more aware of the potential savings in healthcare costs by agreeing to offer these programs and services to employees. Also, the continued integration of physical and health education into school curriculums is crucial, as is the attention to nutrition when negotiating contracts for food services in schools. Finally, government support and funding for community-based obesity-reduction programs—both public and private programs—is crucial to increase awareness and encourage efforts to reduce this problem.

Analyze the essay:

1. In this essay the Center for Urban Policy and the Environment suggests that obesity should be treated as a disease. How do you think the authors of each of the essays in this chapter would respond to this suggestion? Write two or three sentences per author on how they would likely respond.

2. The author suggests that state governments should fund obesity treatment and prevention programs. What do you think: Is it the responsibility of the government to help prevent and treat obesity in Americans? Why or why not? Use evidence from the texts you have read to support your answer.

The Problem of Obesity Is Not a Crisis

Patrick Basham and John Luik

In the following essay Patrick Basham and John Luik argue that the crisis of obesity has been exaggerated. They claim that health officials want to scare the public into believing there is an obesity crisis for two main reasons: to control the lifestyle of citizens, and to charge taxpayers money to fund weight-reduction programs. In the authors' view, very little evidence supports the obesity crisis. They claim that children are not desperately overweight, junk food is not necessarily bad for a person, and being a touch overweight can actually be better for you than constantly dieting. For all of these reasons, Basham and Luik urge the public to resist government fear-mongering that encourages people to think of obesity as a crisis: If a person wants to lose weight, it should be his or her private business.

Basham is director of the Democracy Institute and Luik is a health policy writer whose articles have been published in a variety of publications, including the *Telegraph,* a London newspaper that originally published this essay. Basham and Luik are coauthors of the book *Diet Nation: Exposing the Obesity Crusade.*

Consider the following questions:
1. What are four obesity myths perpetuated by public health officials, in the authors' opinion?
2. What event made normal-sized people in the United States become classified as overweight almost immediately, according to Basham and Luik?
3. What percent of dieters are fatter five years after dieting, as reported by the authors?

Patrick Basham and John Luik, "Four Big, Fat Myths," *Telegraph* (London), November 27, 2006. Reproduced by permission.

Big Brother[1] has an ambition: to become Big Nanny. The [Britain] Government wants to introduce a £224 million [US $440 million] "Children's Index", a massive database of every child in the country, charting progress from birth to adulthood and flagging up "concerns" about each child's development. Two "flags" on a child's record would trigger an official investigation into his or her family.

Not surprisingly, Parliament's Information Commissioner, in a report last week, was highly critical of the scheme. "Government policy proposes treating all parents as if they cannot be trusted to bring up their children," the report said. Increasingly, this is just what the Government and health campaigners believe. One of the proposed danger signs on the Children's Index, after all, would be if the child were not eating the requisite, government-approved amount of fruit and vegetables each day.

The Obesity Epidemic Is a Myth

These health campaigners tell us that British children—and their parents—must be slimmed down because we, like much of the developed world, are in the grip of an obesity epidemic that threatens a health catastrophe. Indeed, the US surgeon general has claimed that obesity is "a greater threat than weapons of mass destruction". The media has picked up on the scares and turned them into a kind of orthodoxy. For instance, the term "childhood obesity" occurred only twice in *The Guardian* in 1999. In 2004, it occurred 201 times, almost four times a week. The public have become convinced that the "epidemic" is a fact.

Yet the obesity epidemic is a myth manufactured by public health officials in concert with assorted academics and special-interest lobbyists. These crusaders preach a sermon consisting of four obesity myths: that we and our

1. "Big Brother" is a term taken from George Orwell's book *1984*. It refers to a watchful, controlling government under which people have few freedoms.

children are fat; that being fat is a certain recipe for early death; that our fatness stems from the manufacturing and marketing practices of the food industry (hence Ofcom's [Office of Communications] recently announced ban on junk food advertising to children); and that we will lengthen our lives if only we eat less and lose weight. The trouble is, there is no scientific evidence to support these myths.

The Childhood Obesity Myth

Let's start with the myth of an epidemic of childhood obesity. The just-published Health Survey for England, 2004 does not show a significant increase in the weight of children in recent years. The Department of Health report found that from 1995 to 2003 there was only a one-pound increase in children's average weight.

One of the principal targets of obesity crusaders is school vending machines.

Nor is there any evidence in claims that overweight and obese children are destined to become overweight and

obese adults. The Thousand Families Study has researched 1,000 Newcastle families since 1954. Researchers have found little connection between overweight children and adult obesity. In the study, four out of five obese people became obese as adults, not as children.

There is not even any compelling scientific evidence to support the Government's claim that childhood obesity results in long-term health problems and lowers one's life expectancy. In fact, the opposite may be true: we could be in danger of creating a generation of children obsessed with their weight with the consequent risk of eating disorders that really do threaten their health. Statistics on the numbers of children with eating disorders are hard to come by, but in the US it is estimated that 10 per cent of high school pupils suffer from them. Recent studies show adults' attempts to control children's eating habits result in children eating more rather than less. Parental finger wagging increases the likelihood that children develop body-image problems as well as eating disorders.

Junk Food Does Not Make Kids Obese

One of the principal targets of the obesity crusaders has been the school vending machine. However, the banning of these machines and their stocks of snacks and sweets is very much at odds with the most recent science on children, junk food, and obesity. In 2004, a World Health Organisation study of 8,904 British pupils found that overweight children ate sweets less frequently than normal-weight children did. Children who ate larger amounts of junk food actually had less chance of being overweight.

One large-scale American study spent three years tracking almost 15,000 boys and girls aged between nine and 14 to investigate the links between body mass index and the consumption of fruit and vegetables. It found no correlation, and concluded that "the recommendation for consumption of fruit and vegetables may be well founded, but should not be based on a beneficial effect on weight regulation".

Body Mass Index Table

Body mass index (BMI) is a tool used to determine the status of a person's weight. To use it, find the place at which your weight and height intersect. Some people argue that BMI values have been inflated to make the public seem fatter than it actually is.

BMI	Normal						Overweight				
	19	20	21	22	23	24	25	26	27	28	29
Height (Feet-Inches)	Weight (pounds)										
4'10"	91	96	100	105	110	115	119	124	129	134	138
4'11"	94	99	104	109	114	119	124	128	133	138	143
5'00"	97	102	107	112	118	123	128	133	138	143	148
5'01"	100	106	111	116	122	127	132	137	143	148	153
5'02"	104	109	115	120	126	131	136	142	147	153	158
5'03"	107	112	118	124	130	135	141	146	152	158	163
5'04"	110	116	122	128	134	140	145	151	157	163	169
5'05"	114	120	126	132	138	144	150	156	162	168	174
5'06"	118	124	130	136	142	148	155	161	167	173	179
5'07"	121	127	134	140	146	153	159	166	172	178	185
5'08"	125	131	138	144	151	158	164	171	177	184	190
5'09"	128	135	142	149	155	162	169	176	182	189	196
5'10"	132	139	146	153	160	167	174	181	188	185	202
5'11"	136	143	150	157	165	172	179	186	193	200	208
6'00"	140	147	154	162	169	177	184	191	199	206	213
6'01"	144	151	159	166	174	182	189	197	204	212	219
6'02"	148	155	163	171	179	186	194	202	210	218	225
6'03"	152	160	168	176	184	192	200	208	216	224	232
6'04"	156	164	172	180	189	197	205	213	221	230	238

Obese										Extreme Obesity		
30	31	32	33	34	35	36	37	38	39	40	41	42
143	148	153	158	162	167	172	177	181	186	191	196	201
148	153	158	163	168	173	178	183	188	193	198	203	208
153	158	163	168	174	179	184	189	194	199	204	209	215
158	164	169	174	180	185	190	195	201	206	211	217	222
164	169	175	180	186	191	196	202	207	213	218	224	229
169	174	180	186	191	197	203	208	214	220	225	231	237
175	180	186	191	197	204	209	215	221	227	232	238	244
180	186	192	196	204	210	216	222	228	234	240	246	252
186	192	198	204	210	216	223	229	235	241	247	253	260
191	198	204	211	217	223	230	236	242	249	255	261	268
197	204	210	216	223	230	236	243	249	256	262	269	276
203	210	216	223	230	236	243	250	257	263	270	277	284
209	216	222	229	236	243	250	257	264	271	278	285	292
215	222	229	236	243	250	257	265	272	279	286	293	301
221	228	235	242	250	258	265	272	279	287	294	302	309
227	235	242	250	258	265	275	280	288	295	302	310	318
233	241	249	256	265	272	280	287	295	303	311	319	326
240	248	256	264	272	279	287	295	303	311	319	327	335
246	254	263	271	279	287	295	304	312	320	328	336	344

Taken from: George Bray, Pennington Biomedical Research Center; *Clinical Guidelines on the Identification, Evaluation, and Treatment of Overweight and Obesity in Adults: The Evidence Report*, National Institutes of Health, National Heart, Lung, and Blood Institute, September 1998.

A False Sense of Overweight

The parallel claim of an adult obesity epidemic is equally unsubstantiated. There has been significant weight gain among the very heaviest segment of the adult population. However, this has not been true of most of the individuals who are labelled overweight and obese, whose weights have only slightly increased. In America, it is true that there was a rapid increase in the number of overweight people in the early years of this decade: but only because the classification of what was "overweight" was reduced from those with a body mass index of 27 to those of 25. Overnight, previously normal weight people discovered they were overweight.

The science linking weight to early death is flimsy, at best. Neither being fat nor moderately obese is associated with increased mortality risks. Last year, a US Centres for Disease Control study found the lowest death rates among overweight people. Furthermore, a study published in the *American Journal of Public Health* found that normal-weight individuals did not outlive their mildly obese counterparts. These findings are replicated in many studies over the past 30 years that have found maximum longevity is associated with being above, rather than below, average weight. . . .

The Problem of Obesity Is Not a Crisis

One night in 1998, 30 million Americans went to bed a "normal" weight and woke up the next morning officially "overweight." It wasn't due to midnight snacking. It was the result of a grand redefinition, which vastly expanded the potential market for prescription diet pills and landed the likes of Will Smith, Pierce Brosnan, Tom Brady, Kobe Bryant and President Bush in the "overweight" category.

Rick Berman, "Industry Salivates over New Cash Cow," *Atlanta Journal Constitution*, February 23, 2005.

Being Overweight Is Not Necessarily Bad

Equally unsupported is the obesity crusaders' campaign for population-wide weight loss. While they try to convince us that we are desperately fat and that our fatness will kill us, the truth about the risks of thinness and the large numbers of thinness-related deaths is quietly ignored. Large numbers of women suffer from anorexia, with one in five hospital cases ending in death. A survey of 5,000 British women in 2000 found that four in 10 had suffered from an eating disorder, such as anorexia or bulimia. These numbers do not take into account the many men and women, neither anorexic nor bulimic, who place themselves at risk through their fixation with dieting.

Contemporary weight gain is not the result of higher food consumption; rather, it reflects a lack of exercise. For the first time in many years, membership of British gyms is in decline. A survey found that most overweight British women seeking to shed pounds choose a fashionable diet over cardiovascular exercise or lifting weights at a gym. Overweight women are more likely to turn to cosmetic surgery, slimming pills or starvation to solve their problems, than to exercise.

Some skeptics argue that being slightly overweight is better for a person's health than being constantly on a diet.

Money Spent on Weight-Loss Programs Is Wasted

But the sad truth is that attempts at weight loss are largely unsuccessful, even in highly controlled situations. Of every 100 people who respond to the crusaders' sermon that they should lose weight, only four will be able to maintain their post-diet weight. Ninety-five per cent of dieters are fatter five years after their diet then when they started to trim.

Weight-loss campaigners also ignore evidence of an association between weight loss and increased mortality. Two American studies—the Iowa Women's Health Study and the American Cancer Society study—found that weight loss was associated with higher rates of mortality. Research following up the ACS study found that healthy obese women were, in fact, better off not losing weight. They were at less risk from cancer and cardiovascular disease than healthy women who dieted.

Obesity crusaders believe that the nanny state has the right to define and enforce a single vision of what constitutes healthy living a good life. The government's judgment is considered inherently superior in any individual's judgment that fatness is at least personally tolerable.

We Must Reject the Nanny Nation

The obesity crusade presumes a nursery nation comprised of docile infant-citizens too uncertain of their own values to be left to make their own way in a world in which an evil Ronald McDonald lurks under every archway. Obesity crusaders believe the individual has an obligation to order his life according to their judgment about health, and that the government may justifiably force him to conform if he demurs.

The lasting legacy of the obesity crusade will be both a much fatter government and a much thinner citizenry.

The government will be fatter through its expanded power to shape inappropriately the lives of its citizens. Britons will be thinner in their capacity for choice, self-government, and personal responsibility.

Analyze the essay:

1. The author of the previous essay, the Center for Urban Policy and the Environment, argues that obesity is a crisis because it causes health problems. How do Patrick Basham and John Luik respond to those claims in this essay? List at least two claims they make on the issue of weight and health. Then, state which author you agree with, and why.

2. In their essay Basham and Luik talk about the "nanny state" and argue it will leave government fatter and citizens thinner. What is the nanny state, and what do they mean by their charge about a fat government and a thin citizenry? Clarify the authors' thoughts and say whether you agree with their concerns.

Being Obese Has Serious Health Risks

Weight-control Information Network

The Weight-control Information Network (WIN) was established in 1994 to provide the general public, health professionals, the media, and Congress with information on obesity, weight control, physical activity, and related nutritional issues. It is a division of the National Institute of Diabetes and Digestive and Kidney Diseases (NIDDKD). In the following essay WIN argues that being obese has many negative health effects. They warn that an overweight person is at increased risk for developing diabetes, heart disease, stroke, cancer, joint disease, gallbladder disease, pregnancy complications, and other diseases. WIN says that people can reduce their risk of most of these diseases by reducing their total body weight by just 5 or 10 percent, and it encourages Americans to improve their health by eating well and exercising.

Consider the following questions:

1. What percent of people with type 2 diabetes are also overweight, according to the author?
2. How much weight loss does WIN say can reduce a person's risk of developing heart disease or having a stroke?
3. Why might being overweight increase a person's risk of cancer, according to WIN?

Weight-control Information Network, "Do You Know the Health Risks of Being Overweight?" win.niddk.nih.gov, October 2007.

Weighing too much may increase your risk for developing many health problems. If you are overweight or obese, you may be at risk for:

- type 2 diabetes
- coronary heart disease and stroke
- metabolic syndrome
- certain types of cancer
- sleep apnea
- osteoarthritis
- gallbladder disease
- fatty liver disease
- pregnancy complications . . .

The Risk of Type 2 Diabetes

Type 2 diabetes is a disease in which blood sugar levels are above normal. High blood sugar is a major cause of coronary heart disease, kidney disease, stroke, amputation, and blindness. In 2002, diabetes was the sixth leading cause of death in the United States.

Type 2 diabetes is the most common type of diabetes in the United States. This form of diabetes is most often associated with old age, obesity, family history of diabetes, previous history of gestational diabetes, and physical inactivity. The disease is more common among certain ethnic populations.

More than 85 percent of people with type 2 diabetes are overweight. It is not known exactly why people who are overweight are more likely to develop this disease. It may be that being overweight causes cells to change, making them resistant to the hormone insulin. Insulin carries sugar from blood to the cells, where it is used for energy. When a person is insulin resistant, blood sugar cannot be taken up by the cells, resulting in high blood sugar. In addition, the cells that produce insulin must work extra hard to try to keep blood sugar normal. This may cause these cells to gradually fail.

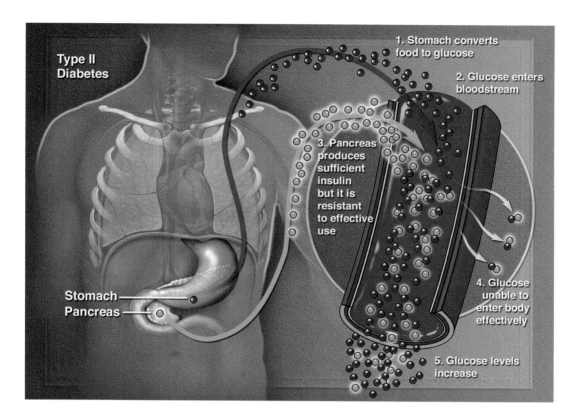

Type II Diabetes

1. Stomach converts food to glucose

2. Glucose enters bloodstream

3. Pancreas produces sufficient insulin but it is resistant to effective use

4. Glucose unable to enter body effectively

5. Glucose levels increase

Stomach

Pancreas

Type 2 diabetes is a disease in which blood sugar levels are above normal and is a major cause of coronary heart disease, stroke, and kidney disease.

Losing Weight Helps

You may lower your risk for developing type 2 diabetes by losing weight and increasing the amount of physical activity you do. If you have type 2 diabetes, losing weight and becoming more physically active can help you control your blood sugar levels and prevent or delay complications. Losing weight and exercising more may also allow you to reduce the amount of diabetes medication you take. The Diabetes Prevention Program, a large clinical study sponsored by the National Institutes of Health, found that losing just 5 to 7 percent of your body weight and doing moderate-intensity exercise for 30 minutes a day, 5 days a week, may prevent or delay the onset of type 2 diabetes. . . .

Obesity, Heart Disease, and Stroke

People who are overweight are more likely to develop high blood pressure, high levels of triglycerides (blood fats) and LDL cholesterol (a fat-like substance often called "bad cholesterol"), and low levels of HDL cholesterol ("good cholesterol"). These are all risk factors for heart disease and stroke. In addition, excess body fat—especially abdominal fat—may produce substances that cause inflammation. Inflammation in blood vessels and throughout the body may raise heart disease risk.

Losing 5 to 10 percent of your weight can lower your chances for developing coronary heart disease or having a stroke. If you weigh 200 pounds, this means losing as little as 10 pounds. Weight loss may improve blood pressure, triglyceride, and cholesterol levels; improve heart function and blood flow; and decrease inflammation throughout the body.

Cancer: The Second Leading Cause of Death in the United States

Cancer occurs when cells in one part of the body, such as the colon, grow abnormally or out of control. The cancerous cells sometimes spread to other parts of the body, such as the liver. Cancer is the second leading cause of death in the United States.

Being overweight may increase the risk of developing several types of cancer, including cancers of the colon, esophagus, and kidney. Overweight is also linked with uterine and post-menopausal breast cancer in women. Gaining weight during adult life increases the risk for several of these cancers, even if the weight gain does not result in overweight or obesity.

It is not known exactly how being overweight increases cancer risk. It may be that fat cells release hormones that affect cell growth, leading to cancer. Also, eating or physical activity habits that may lead to being overweight may also contribute to cancer risk.

Being Obese Has Serious Health Risks

The health problems that stem from being overweight go way beyond the ones we usually hear about, like diabetes and heart disease. Being overweight can also affect a person's joints, breathing, sleep, mood, and energy levels. So being overweight can impact a person's entire quality of life.

Mary L. Gavin, ed., "When Being Overweight Is a Health Problem," Nemours Foundation, 2007.

Obesity Increases a Person's Risk of Disease

States with the highest obesity rates are among the states with the highest rates of diabetes and hypertension, two of several obesity-related diseases.

States with Highest Obesity Rates

Ranking	State	Percentage of Adult Obesity (Based on 2004–2006 Combined Data, Including Confidence Intervals)
1	Mississippi	30.6% (+/- 0.9)
2	West Virginia	29.8% (+/- 1.0)
3	Alabama	29.4% (+/- 1.2)
4	Louisiana	28.2% (+/- 0.9)
5 (tie)	South Carolina	27.8% (+/- 0.7)
5 (tie)	Tennessee	27.8% (+/- 1.2)
7	Kentucky	27.5% (+/- 1.0)
8	Arkansas	27.0% (+/- 0.9)
9 (tie)	Indiana	26.8% (+/- 0.8)
9 (tie)	Michigan	26.8% (+/- 0.8)
9 (tie)	Oklahoma	26.8% (+/- 0.8)
12 (tie)	Missouri	26.3% (+/- 1.0)
12 (tie)	Texas	26.3% (+/- 0.9)
14	Georgia	26.1% (+/- 1.0)
15	Ohio	26.0% (+/- 1.2)

States with Highest Rates of Adult Diabetes

Ranking	State	Percentage of Adult Diabetes (Based on 2004–2006 Combined Data, Including Confidence Intervals)	Ranking
1	West Virginia	11.1% (+/- 1.0)	2
2	Mississippi	10.1% (+/- 0.5)	1
3 (tie)	South Carolina	9.4% (+/- 0.4)	5 (tie)
3 (tie)	Tennessee	9.4% (+/- 0.6)	5 (tie)
5	Alabama	9.3% (+/- 0.6)	3
6	Oklahoma	9.0% (+/- 0.4)	9
7	Louisiana	8.9% (+/- 0.5)	4
8	Kentucky	8.8% (+/- 0.5)	7
9	North Carolina	8.7% (+/- 0.3)	17
10	Florida	8.4% (+/- 0.5)	34

States with Highest Rates of Adult Hypertension

Ranking	State	Percentage of Adult Hypertension (Based on 2001–2005 Combined Data, Including Confidence Intervals) Based on a Survey Conducted Every Other Year	Ranking
1	Mississippi	32.7% (+/- 1.0)	1
2	West Virginia	32.5% (+/- 1.0)	2
3	Alabama	32.0% (+/- 1.1)	3
4	Tennessee	29.9% (+/- 1.1)	5 (tie)
5	Arkansas	29.8% (+/- 0.9)	8
6	South Carolina	29.7% (+/- 0.8)	5 (tie)
7	Kentucky	29.4% (+/- 0.9)	7
8	Oklahoma	28.8% (+/- 0.8)	9
9	Louisiana	28.6% (+/- 0.9)	4
10	North Carolina	28.4% (+/- 0.8)	17

Taken from: Jeffrey Levi, Emily Gadola, and Laura M. Segal, "F as in Fat: How Obesity Policies Are Failing in America," Trust for America's Health, August 2007. http://healthyamericans.org/reports/obesity2007/Report.pdf.

Avoiding weight gain may prevent a rise in cancer risk. Healthy eating and physical activity habits may lower cancer risk. Weight loss may also lower your risk, although studies have been inconclusive. . . .

Being Overweight Strains the Body

Osteoarthritis is a common joint disorder that causes the joint bone and cartilage (tissue that protects joints) to wear away. Osteoarthritis most often affects the joints of the knees, hips, and lower back.

Extra weight may place extra pressure on joints and cartilage, causing them to wear away. In addition, people with more body fat may have higher blood levels of substances that cause inflammation. Inflammation at the joints may raise the risk for osteoarthritis.

Weight loss of at least 5 percent of your body weight may decrease stress on your knees, hips, and lower back, and lessen inflammation in your body. If you have osteoarthritis, losing weight may help improve your symptoms.

An Increased Risk of Gallbladder Disease

Gallbladder disease includes gallstones and inflammation or infection of the gallbladder. Gallstones are clusters of solid material that form in the gallbladder. They are made mostly of cholesterol and can cause abdominal pain, especially after consuming fatty foods. The pain may be sharp or dull.

People who are overweight have a higher risk for developing gallbladder disease. They may produce more cholesterol (a fat-like substance found in the body), a risk factor for gallstones. Also, people who are overweight may have an enlarged gallbladder, which may not work properly.

Fast weight loss (more than 3 pounds per week) or large weight loss can actually increase your chance of developing gallstones. Modest, slow weight loss of about 1/2 to 2 pounds a week is less likely to cause gallstones. Achieving a healthy weight may lower your risk for developing gallstones. . . .

Pregnancy Complication

Overweight and obesity raise the risk of pregnancy complications for both mother and baby. Pregnant women who are overweight or obese may have an increased risk for:

- Gestational diabetes (high blood sugar during pregnancy).
- Pre-eclampsia (high blood pressure during pregnancy that can cause severe problems for both mother and baby if left untreated).
- Cesarean delivery or complications with cesarean delivery.

Babies of overweight or obese mothers have an increased risk of neural tube defects (defects of the brain and spinal cord), stillbirth, prematurity, and being large for gestational age.

Pregnant women who are overweight are more likely to develop insulin resistance, high blood sugar, and high blood pressure. (Insulin resistance is when cells do not respond properly to the hormone insulin, which carries

Eating well and exercising regularly helps keep people at a normal weight, which may lower their risk of developing cancer.

blood sugar to cells for energy. It may result in high levels of blood sugar.) Overweight also increases the risks associated with surgery and anesthesia, and severe obesity increases operative time and blood loss.

Some studies have shown that gaining excess weight during pregnancy—even without becoming obese—may increase risks. It is important to consult with your obstetrician or other health care provider about how much weight to gain during pregnancy. . . .

Weight Loss Reduces the Risk of Disease

Losing excess weight after delivery may help women reduce their health risks. If a woman developed gestational diabetes, losing weight will lower her risk of developing diabetes later in life.

If you are overweight, losing as little as 5 percent of your body weight may lower your risk for several diseases.

Analyze the essay:

1. The author of this essay, the Weight-control Information Network (WIN), is part of the National Institute of Diabetes and Digestive and Kidney Diseases (NIDDKD), which is one of the National Institutes of Health. Does the fact that this essay was written by a government organization influence the degree to which you take it seriously? Why or why not?

2. The author of the following essay, Paul Campos, challenges claims made by WIN about the health risks of being overweight and obese. What evidence does he use to do this? After reading both essays, what is your opinion on the health risks of being overweight and obese? Support your answer with evidence from the texts.

The Health Risks of Obesity Are Exaggerated

Paul Campos

In the following essay Paul Campos argues that the health risks of being obese and overweight have been greatly exaggerated. He casts doubt on studies that have shown a link between being overweight and developing a risk for certain diseases, saying that the studies do not take into account other factors—such as lifestyle or income— that might contribute to a person's risk of developing a disease. Furthermore, he claims that being overweight is not bad for one's health. Numerous studies have shown that it is healthier to be overweight than underweight, and Campos says that being overweight can reduce one's risk of developing certain diseases, such as Alzheimer's and Parkinson's disease. Campos attributes misinformation about obesity and health to a citizenry that refuses to believe what on the surface seems illogical. He calls on the media and public health officials to responsibly deliver news about obesity and health so that Americans scale back their irrational fear of being overweight.

Campos is a professor of law at the University of Colorado.

Consider the following questions:

1. Name six explanations other than being obese that Campos offers for a person who has been defined as obese dying from a heart attack.
2. What did a study by Katherine Flegal conclude about overweight and health?
3. According to Campos, who is at a greater health risk: a 110-pound woman or a 150-pound woman? Why?

Paul Campos, "Don't Feed the Humans!" *New Republic*, November 27, 2007. Reproduced by permission of *The New Republic*.

The reaction of America's leading "obesity" experts to the latest study on the issue demonstrates yet again that our current definition of the word "overweight" makes no sense. Walter Willett of the Harvard School of Public Health's fumed that the new findings were "rubbish." His colleague JoAnn Manson found the study, authored by Katherine Flegal and others, and published in the prestigious *Journal of the American Medical Association*, "very puzzling." After all, for "overweight" people to be healthier than "healthy weight" people just doesn't seem logically or linguistically possible.

How did we get into this mess? First, the relevant definitions: According to public health authorities in America and around the world, people are "overweight" if they have a body mass index between 25 and 30 (for a 5'4" woman this is between 145 and 173 pounds; a 5'10" man fits the category if he weighs between 174 and 208 pounds).

An Absurd Definition of Obesity

A decade ago, when I began to study the relationship between weight and health, I was struck by the almost total lack of medical justification for labeling people in this weight range "overweight." Since then, the situation has become considerably more absurd. It's possible to have reasonable disagreements about the extent to which "obesity" (defined as a BMI of 30 or higher) is an independent contributor to ill-health and mortality risk. After all, epidemiology is a crude science, and the correlations between ill health and body weight among very fat people are inevitably open to multiple interpretations.

For example, suppose one follows two groups, each made up of 5,000 people, for ten years. People in the first group are at their supposed "ideal weight" for their height, while people in the second group are "obese." After a decade, twenty people in the first group and thirty in the second have died of heart disease. Statistically, this means the fat people had a 50% increased risk of dying from heart disease than the thin people did. (This is

Some studies have shown that people who are overweight have, on average, better overall health and lower mortality rates than people who are underweight.

typical of the sorts of risk ratios associated with obesity, and an example of how a handful of extra deaths, in the context of a tiny baseline risk, makes for scary-sounding headlines about obesity "raising the risk of a fatal heart attack by 50%.") Does that mean the ten extra heart disease deaths were *caused* by fatness? Far from it. Perhaps the fat people were, on average, poorer; more stressed; more prone to diet and therefore to weight cycle; more likely to use diet drugs, many of which have been linked to cardiovascular disease; more sedentary; more discriminated against by the health care system and by society in general; and so on. Long-term observational studies of this sort can never control for more than a few of these sort of confounding variables, making it difficult to determine the extent to which, if at all, a particular correlation between a risk factor and a health outcome is causal.

Overweight People Tend to Be Healthier

But all this involves a very different question from that at the center of the controversy over whether being "overweight" is unhealthy. Flegal's study has provided yet another rigorous demonstration of the fact that, if anything, people in the "overweight" category have, on average, better overall health and lower mortality rates than people in the absurdly mislabeled "healthy weight" category.

Flegal and her colleagues found that, for a whole range of diseases, from Alzheimer's and Parkinson's to infectious illness and most of the major respiratory ailments, "overweight" people face a lower mortality risk than "healthy weight" persons. In addition, they found no difference between the two groups in mortality risk from heart disease or cancer (the nation's two biggest killers, and ones that many people tend to associate with being overweight). Thus, the relative mortality risk, and by extension the overall health, of "overweight" Americans appears to be better than that of "healthy weight" people.

In the context of America's war on fat, the fact that being called "overweight" makes no medical or scientific sense is hardly a trivial point. How do our anti-fat warriors deal with this inconvenient truth?

People Who Are Underweight Face Health Risks

Three rationalizations are getting prominent play. First, obesity researchers point out that while being overweight doesn't correlate with increased health risk, being obese does, and "overweight" people are closer to being "obese" than "healthy weight." "You should not take heart in the idea that if you are only overweight you are OK . . . because people gain weight as they age in this country," said Robert

Kushner, a professor of medicine at Northwestern. The problem with this argument is that, statistically speaking, people who are even slightly "underweight" face greatly increased health risks. Consider two women of average height, who weigh 110 and 150 pounds, respectively. The former "ideal weight" woman is roughly ten pounds away from a lower weight level that correlates with a doubling of her mortality risk, while the latter "overweight" woman would have to gain more than 100 pounds to move into a similar risk category. And while people generally gain weight in middle age, they usually begin to lose weight once they've reached retirement age—and nearly 80% of all deaths take place among people 65 and older. (Indeed, high weight has almost no correlation—or even a negative correlation— with mortality risk among the elderly, while weight loss has a very strong positive correlation, even when one controls for weight loss caused by eventually fatal illnesses.) Given these facts, it seems odd to focus on the possibility of an "overweight" woman gaining 100 pounds rather than a thin woman losing ten.

> ## The Health Risks of Obesity Are Exaggerated
>
> We do no service to the people at risk of obesity-related morbidities in our society by "hyping" their plight, exaggerating their numbers or diverting limited educational, medical and financial resources away from where the problems really lie.
>
> Social Issues Research Centre, "Obesity and the Facts," February 2005. www.sirc.org/obesity/obesityfacts.pdf.

Exaggerations and Bogus Ideals

Second, researchers talk about "quality of life." After all, life expectancy isn't everything. As Manson says, "health extends far beyond mortality rates." According to a *New York Times* story, Manson is concerned that excess weight makes it difficult for people to move around, and therefore impairs their quality of life. That's part of "the big picture in terms of health outcomes," Manson says. The notion that an average-height woman who weighs between 146 and 175 pounds is going to find it difficult to move about is as good an example as one could hope to find

The scientific definition of what constitutes an "ideal weight" is complicated by the fact that people generally gain weight in middle age but lose it as they become elderly.

of what eating disorder experts call "anorexic ideation." Here again, we see how an argument which may make sense when talking about extremely fat people is transferred onto people who are "fat" only in the sense that they don't conform to a radical preference for extreme thinness—a preference which is one of the key explanations for why we're saddled with a scientifically bogus definition of what constitutes a "healthy weight."

Finally, as a senior government scientist told me last week, "There's this new argument going around that says overweight people are living longer because they're going to the doctor more often and are therefore getting better medical care." The scientist emphasized that, in a culture where access to medical care is closely linked to socio-economic status, and in which socio-economic status is inversely related to increasing body mass, this argument is, to put it politely, highly implausible.

Let's Believe the Obvious: Obesity Has Been Exaggerated

Still, when the entire public health establishment has put its stamp of approval on a definition, those who have staked their professional reputations on the accuracy of that definition aren't going to be deterred by something like, well, evidence. Predictably, Willett, who has been perhaps the most prominent proponent of the idea that people ought to try to maintain very low weights, was outraged by the latest refutation of his theories: "It's just ludicrous to say there is no increased risk of mortality from being overweight," he told *The Washington Post*.

What's actually ludicrous is that Occam's razor[1] has yet to be employed to explain the "very puzzling" result that, once again, "overweight" people have been found to enjoy better health than "healthy weight" people. The definition of "overweight" promulgated by Willett, Manson, and their colleagues makes no sense. Many "puzzling" results cease to puzzle when one stops abusing the English language.

Analyze the essay:

1. Paul Campos quotes from several sources to support the points he makes in his essay. Make a list of everyone he quotes, including their credentials and the nature of their comments. Then, analyze his sources—are they credible? Are they well qualified to speak on this subject?

2. Campos suggests that studies that link obesity with health problems might be conducted in a way that provides a false explanation for a problem. What do you think: How useful are statistics when trying to determine the cause of a problem? Explain your reasoning.

1. Occam's razor is the principle that essentially says, "all things being equal, the simplest solution is usually the best."

The Government Is Responsible for Helping People Lose Weight

Jeffrey Levi, Emily Gadola, and Laura M. Segal

Trust for America's Health (TFAH) is an organization whose goal is to make disease prevention a national priority. TFAH considers obesity to be a disease and argues that the government should take significant steps to reduce obesity in Americans. In the following essay, TFAH researchers Jeffrey Levi, Emily Gadola, and Laura M. Segal propose creating a National Strategy to Combat Obesity. This government plan would incorporate officials from every federal government agency and task them with helping Americans to eat better and exercise more. The authors consider obesity to be a national threat similar to a flu pandemic and thus believe all sectors of government should work together to protect Americans from the health and economic risks of obesity. They conclude that Americans are not able to fight obesity on their own and need the government's help to thwart the health risks of obesity and to reject health-compromising foods and habits.

Consider the following questions:

1. How does obesity hurt American business prospects, in the authors' opinion?
2. What changes do the authors suggest making to schools to promote more physical activity among American children?
3. What should restaurants and food companies be required to provide, according to the authors?

Jeffrey Levi, Emily Gadola, and Laura M. Segal, "F as in Fat: How Obesity Policies Are Failing in America," Trust for America's Health, August 2007. Reproduced by permission.

Obesity has dominated media headlines over the past few years as the nation has begun to recognize it is a serious health crisis.

Two-thirds of American adults are obese or overweight, and in the past year, obesity rates have continued to rise in 31 states. Eighty-five percent of Americans believe that obesity is an epidemic, according to a new poll conducted by Trust for America's Health (TFAH).

Poor nutrition and physical inactivity are increasing Americans' risk for developing major diseases, including type 2 diabetes, heart disease and stroke and some forms of cancer. But while the obesity epidemic has garnered increased attention, a comparable increase in action has yet to occur.

While many promising efforts are being initiated across the country, there is no national commitment to addressing the problem. . . .

National Action Is Needed

The country needs to develop a plan for combating obesity that is in proportion to the scope and depth of the problem. This will require focusing on strategies that will work on a wide scale. The question is, is America willing to make the commitment needed to return to better health?

Today's children are likely to be the first generation to live shorter, less healthy lives than their parents. Approximately 25 million children are already obese or overweight.

The crisis has an impact beyond individual health. U.S. economic competitiveness is hurting as our workforce becomes less healthy and productive. Obesity related health care costs are draining dollars from the bottom line of businesses.

Widespread Changes Needed

The future health of the country requires us to invest in changes that will make it easier to help people make healthier choices.

Anti-obesity advocates think the federal government should become more involved in a national strategy to combat obesity.

These include making changes to our schools, our workplaces, our homes and our communities. The crisis requires everyone to engage: government at all levels, businesses—big and small, health care providers, community groups, and families. . . .

A National Strategy to Combat Obesity

The federal government should develop and implement a National Strategy to Combat Obesity. This plan should involve every federal government agency, define clear roles and responsibilities for states and localities, and engage private industry and community groups.

Every segment of society has a role to play in fighting the epidemic, including families, health care providers, schools, businesses, and communities. Political will must be galvanized to make combating obesity a national priority at all levels of government.

State and local health departments should convene diverse local leaders and members of the community to look for ways to promote physical activity and healthy eating, making information available and making changes that help make it easier for people to make healthier choices.

Let's Dedicate the Government to Fighting Obesity

Our national leaders should give the crisis the attention it deserves by developing the National Strategy to Combat Obesity. The National Strategy for Pandemic Influenza Preparedness, with comprehensive government-wide responsibilities, clear timelines, and detailed action items, provides a strong example for how this type of effort could be undertaken. Obesity is as much of a threat to the public's health as the looming possibility of a flu pandemic, and the nation must make a similar level of commitment by creating a government-wide plan for addressing the problem and providing the funding needed to carry out the plan.

As part of the strategy the nation's health officials should articulate federal government-wide responsibilities across multiple Departments (e.g. Health and Human Services, Transportation, Agriculture, Education, Interior), provide specific responsibilities to states and localities, define expectations of the private sector, develop detailed guidelines, action items, benchmarks, and timelines.

The federal government must provide significant funding for implementation of the National Strategy to Combat Obesity. This must include investment to increase both scientific research to develop effective, wide-scale public health solutions and to provide communities with the capacity and resources needed to make changes. The federal government needs to make a serious national commitment to this public health crisis, instead of the fits-and-starts and funding-and-cutting pattern we have today.

Federal agencies must put forward clear, consistent recommendations for nutrition and physical activity for individuals. Currently, CDC [Centers for Disease Control and Prevention] NIH [National Institutes for Health] and the *Dietary Guidelines for Americans, 2005*, all have slight variations on physical activity recommendations. Information about healthy eating and activity should be contained in a single set of clear guidelines and promoted through high profile and ongoing public education efforts. . . .

Helping All Americans Become More Physically Active

Research shows even small amounts of physical activity can lead to major improvements in health. Americans must be given the tools they need to engage in more physical activity. In addition, children should be given the opportunity to be more physically active throughout the day, both in and out of school. The communities we live in should allow greater opportunities for physical activity, including places for safe and affordable public recreation and increased availability of sidewalks.

With the rise in childhood obesity, special attention should be given to finding ways to help young people to habitually make physical activity a part of their daily lives. While schools and school districts are struggling to meet set academic standards with limited resources and time, physical education is often being squeezed out. School design and community planning and development are also creating obstacles to physical activity in everyday life.

What Schools Should Do

Steps to improve opportunities for physical activity include:

- Federal, state and local governments need to make sure that physical education is part of the curriculum in every school. This includes eliminating barriers to physical education, such as lack of quality teachers or insufficient funding.

- Schools should be encouraged to not only increase the amount of time students spend in physical education classes but ensure that enough time is actually being spent in moderate-to-vigorous physical activity before and after school and between classes.
- Schools and communities should ensure that their environments are conducive to improving physical activity in children (e.g., establish safe routes to schools, work with city or county to have well-marked crosswalks and sidewalks for safe walking and cycling). The need for physical activity should be incorporated into all planning for building new schools or remodeling existing schools.

The Public Wants the Government to Fight Obesity

According to a 2007 report, the majority of Americans believe it is the government's responsibility to fight obesity. Support for government weight-reduction programs is especially high among Americans who earn less than $50,000 per year (per household).

Support for government role in combating obesity by income level	Percent government should have role
Total	81
Less than $30,000/yr household	87
$30,000–$50,000/yr household	85
$50,000–$75,000/yr household	80
More than $75,000/yr household	77

Taken from: Jeffrey Levi, Emily Gadola, and Laura M. Segal, "F as in Fat: How Obesity Policies Are Failing in America," Trust for America's Health, August 2007. http://healthyamericans.org/reports/obesity2007/Report.pdf.

Advocates say that as part of a national strategy against obesity schools should be encouraged to increase student time spent in physical education classes.

Helping Americans Choose Healthier Foods

Americans must be given the tools to take personal responsibility for their eating habits, including nutritional recommendations, access to supermarkets, nutritional information when they purchase food, and healthy food in schools.

Addressing growing obesity rates is going to require Americans to dramatically change their eating habits. Instead of periodically cutting calories or going on fad diets, individuals need to develop healthy and balanced diets to complement a more physically active lifestyle.

Public Education Is Needed

Information about healthy eating and physical activity should be promoted through high profile and ongoing public education efforts. And, while the *Dietary Guidelines for Americans, 2005* provide recommendations for healthy eating, there needs to be greater acknowledgement that the American diet is extremely different from those recommendations, so greater effort needs to be made to bridge the divide.

Improving America's nutrition requires the following steps:

- USDA should require all schools to meet the *Dietary Guidelines for Americans, 2005* and should implement IOM nutrition standards for "competitive foods" in schools.
- Provide nutrition counseling as part of preventive health services covered by insurance.
- Require restaurants and food companies to provide better and more readily accessible information about the nutritional content of their products.
- Implement an overall U.S. agricultural policy that works to improve Americans' nutrition choices and increase opportunities for fruit and vegetable consumption.
- Improve access to healthy foods in all communities and schools, especially communities that face additional barriers (e.g. lack of grocery stores).

Analyze the essay:

1. In this essay the authors say obesity is as much a threat to public health as is the threat of a flu pandemic. How do you think the other authors in this section might respond to this claim? Write two or three sentences per author explaining how they would likely respond.

2. The author of the following essay, William Saletan, argues that it is not the government's job to help people lose weight. The authors of this essay disagree. After reading both essays, what place do you think the government should have in fighting obesity? Do Americans need the government's help to eat healthy and exercise frequently, or should the responsibility fall on their own shoulders? Support your answer using evidence from the texts you have read.

The Government Is Not Responsible for Helping People Lose Weight

William Saletan

In the following essay William Saletan argues it is not the government's job to help Americans lose weight. Having won the war on smoking, Saletan accuses health officials of looking for a new scapegoat for health problems. They have chosen to wage war on junk food and obesity, despite Saletan's claim that food is not a worthy enemy. Food keeps us alive and is a source of sustenance, nourishment, and enjoyment. Saletan says the politicians, lawyers, and health crusaders will have a harder time making a target out of food than they have other so-called menaces, such as cigarettes and alcohol. He concludes that it is not the government's job to tell people what to eat and urges Americans to resist being taken in by a war waged on food.

Saletan is a national correspondent for *Slate*, the online news magazine from which this essay was taken. He is also the author of *Bearing Right: How Conservatives Won the Abortion War*.

Consider the following questions:

1. What natural disaster did federal officials compare obesity to, according to Saletan?
2. What percent of Americans view fast-food companies unfavorably, according to a 2005 Pew Research poll?
3. What does the author mean when he says it is ridiculous to treat milk, French fries, and pizza like soda, jelly beans, and gum?

William Saletan, "Junk-Food Jihad: Should We Regulate French Fries Like Cigarettes?" Slate.com, April 15, 2006. Distributed by United Feature Syndicate, Inc.

Goodbye, war on smoking. Hello, war on fat.

In a span of two months, smoking bans have been imposed in Scotland, enacted in England, Denmark, and Uruguay, proposed by the government of Portugal, and endorsed by the French public. China has banned new cigarette factories. In Virginia, our third most prolific tobacco state, senators voted to ban smoking in nearly all public places. The Arkansas legislature, backed by a Republican governor, passed a similar ban and voted to extend this policy to cars in which a child is present. Tobacco companies have won a skirmish here or there, but always in retreat.

Obesity Is the New Enemy

So, we've found a new enemy: obesity. [In 2004], the government discovered that the targets of previous crusades—booze, sex, guns, and cigarettes—were killing a smaller percentage of Americans than they used to. The one thing you're not allowed to do in a culture war is win it, so we searched the mortality data for the next big menace. The answer was as plain as the other chin on your face. Obesity, federal officials told us, would soon surpass tobacco as the chief cause of preventable death. They compared it to the Black Death and the Asian tsunami. They sent a team of "disease detectives" to West Virginia to investigate an obesity outbreak. [In March 2006], the surgeon general called obesity "the terror within" and said it would "dwarf 9-11."

How do we fight it? Everyone agrees on exercising and eating responsibly. The debate is over what the government should do. Health advocates want to restrict junk-food sales, regulate advertising, require more explicit labels, and ban trans fats (also known as partially hydrogenated oils), which are often put into crackers, cookies, and other products to prolong shelf life. They marshal the kind of evidence that won the war on smoking: correlations between soda, junk food, obesity, disease, and death. Lawyers who made their fortunes suing tobacco companies are preparing suits against soda companies.

Anti-obesity advocates want the government to restrict junk food sales, regulate advertising, and ban certain food ingredients. Others say the government should stay out of the debate.

[In February 2006], when President [George W.] Bush gave a health-care speech at the headquarters of [fast-foot restaurant] Wendy's, activists compared the hamburger chain to [tobacco company] Philip Morris. They see themselves as waging the same brave struggle, this time against "the food industry."

Declaring War on . . . Food?

But somehow, "the food industry" doesn't sound quite as evil as "the tobacco industry." Something about food—the fact that it keeps us alive, perhaps—makes its purveyors hard to hate. For that matter, the rationale for recent bans on smoking is the injustice of secondhand smoke, and there's no such thing as secondhand obesity. [In 2005,] a Pew Research poll found that 74 percent of Americans viewed tobacco companies unfavorably, but only 39 percent viewed fast-food companies unfavorably. [In April 2006,] a Pew survey found that more Americans blame obesity, especially their own, on lack of exercise and willpower than on "the kinds of foods marketed at restaurants and grocery stores."

These obstacles don't make the assault on junk food futile. But they do clarify how it will unfold. It will rely on three arguments: First, we should protect kids. Second, fat people are burdening the rest of us. Third, junk food isn't really food.

The War on Food Begins with Kids

Targeting kids is a familiar way to impose morals without threatening liberties. You can have a beer or an abortion, but your daughter can't. The conservative aspect of this argument is that you're entitled, as a parent, to decide what your kids can do or buy. That's the pitch Sen. Tom Harkin, D-Iowa, made [in April 2006] in a bill to crack down on junk food in schools. The liberal half of the argument is that kids are too young to make informed choices. In this case, it's true. Studies show that little kids ask for products they see on television; fail to distinguish ads from programs; and are heavily targeted by companies peddling candy, fast food, and sugared cereal.

This stage of the fat war will be a rout. In schools, the audience is young and captive, and the facts are appalling. According to a government report, 75 percent of high schools, 65 percent of middle schools, and 30 percent of elementary schools have contracts with "beverage"—i.e., soda—companies. The sodas are commonly sold through vending machines. The contracts stipulate how many thousands of cases each district has

> ## The Government Is Not Responsible for Helping Lose Weight
>
> Regulating food portions to outlawing unhealthy ingredients like trans fats to creating "health zones" to taxing certain undesirable foods . . . accelerate[s] the nanny state. If we can ban one ingredient, why not every unhealthy ingredient? If we can tax a candy bar, why not a steak? There lies the danger.
>
> David Harsanyi, interview by Nick Gillespie, "Nanny State 911!" *Reason*, September 28, 2007. www.reason.com/news/show/122716.html.

Many soda companies have contracts with more than 55 percent of America's schools and share some profits with school districts.

to buy, and they offer schools a bigger cut of the profits from soda than from juice or water. Soda companies, realizing they're going to lose this fight, are fleeing elementary schools and arguing that high-schoolers are old enough to choose. But health advocates refuse to draw such a line. They're not going to stop with kids.

It Is Not the Government's Job to Protect Us from Food

To keep junk food away from adults, fat-fighters will have to explain why obesity is the government's business. Some say the government created the problem by subsidizing pork, sugar, cream, high-fructose corn syrup, and other crud. Harkin reasons that the government pays for school lunches and must protect this "investment." But their main argument is that obesity inflates health-care costs and hurts the economy through disability and lost productivity. [In March 2006,] former President [Bill] Clinton, a confessed overeater, told the nation's governors that obesity has caused more than a quarter of the rise in health-care costs since 1987 and threatens our economic competitiveness. It's not our dependence on foreign oil that's killing us. It's our dependence on vegetable oil.

If the fat-fighters win that argument, they'll reach the final obstacle: the sanctity of food. Food is a basic need and a human right. Marlboros [cigarettes] won't keep you alive on a desert island, but Fritos will. To lower junk food to the level of cigarettes, its opponents must persuade you that it isn't really food. They're certainly trying. Soda isn't sustenance, they argue; it's "liquid candy." Crackers aren't baked; they're "engineered," like illegal drugs, to addict people. [In 2005], New York City's health commissioner asked restaurants to stop using trans fats, which he likened to asbestos. But he ignored saturated fats, which are equally bad and more pervasive. Why are trans fats an easier whipping-cream boy? Because they're mostly artificial.

This, I suspect, is where the war will end. Ban all the creepy-soft processed cookies you want to, but respect nature and nutrition. New York City is purging whole milk from its schools, despite the fact that milk has steadily lost market share to soda during the obesity surge. A fact sheet from Harkin implies that schools should treat milk,

French fries, and pizza like soda, jelly beans, and gum. Come on. How many people died in the Irish jelly bean famine? How many babies have nursed on 7-Up? How many food groups does gum share with pizza? If you can't tell the difference, don't tell us what to eat.

Analyze the essay:

1. In his essay Saletan takes issue with people who have characterized obesity as a problem that is as big as the September 11 terrorist attacks. What do you think? Do you agree with Saletan that people who liken obesity to terror are exaggerating, or do you think that obesity is a major problem with the potential to claim thousands of lives? Use evidence from the texts you have read to support your answer.

2. To make his point that it is not the government's job to protect people from obesity, Saletan uses sarcasm and humor, and even name-calling. List a few examples of these techniques and discuss whether you think it is an effective persuasion tactic.

Section Two: Model Essays and Writing Exercises

The Five-Paragraph Essay

An *essay* is a short piece of writing that discusses or analyzes one topic. The five-paragraph essay is a form commonly used in school assignments and tests. Every five-paragraph essay begins with an *introduction*, ends with a *conclusion*, and features three *supporting paragraphs* in the middle.

The Thesis Statement. The introduction includes the essay's thesis statement. The thesis statement presents the argument or point the author is trying to make about the topic. The essays in this book all have different thesis statements because they are making different arguments about obesity.

The thesis statement should clearly tell the reader what the essay will be about. A focused thesis statement helps determine what will be in the essay; the subsequent paragraphs are spent developing and supporting its argument.

The Introduction. In addition to presenting the thesis statement, a well-written introductory paragraph captures the attention of the reader and explains why the topic being explored is important. It may provide the reader with background information on the subject matter or feature an anecdote that illustrates a point relevant to the topic. It could also present startling information that clarifies the point of the essay or puts forth a contradictory position that the essay will refute. Further techniques for writing an introduction are found later in this section.

The Supporting Paragraphs. The introduction is followed by three (or more) supporting paragraphs. These are the main body of the essay. Each paragraph presents and develops a *subtopic* that supports the essay's thesis statement. Each subtopic is spearheaded by a *topic sentence* and supported by its own facts, details, and examples. The writer can use various kinds of supporting material and details to back up the topic of each supporting paragraph. These may include statistics, quotations from people with special knowledge or expertise, historic facts, and anecdotes. A rule of writing is that specific and concrete examples are more convincing than vague, general, or unsupported assertions.

The Conclusion. The conclusion is the paragraph that closes the essay. Its function is to summarize or reiterate the main idea of the essay. It may recall an idea from the introduction or briefly examine the larger implications of the thesis. Because the conclusion is also the last chance a writer has to make an impression on the reader, it is important that it not simply repeat what has been presented elsewhere in the essay but close it in a clear, final, and memorable way.

Although the order of the essay's component paragraphs is important, they do not have to be written in the order presented here. Some writers like to decide on a thesis and write the introduction paragraph first. Other writers like to focus first on the body of the essay, and write the introduction and conclusion later.

Pitfalls to Avoid

When writing essays about controversial issues such as obesity, it is important to remember that disputes over the material are common precisely because there are many different perspectives. Remember to state your arguments in careful and measured terms. Evaluate your topic fairly—avoid overstating negative qualities of one perspective or understating positive qualities of another. Use examples, facts, and details to support any assertions you make.

The Persuasive Essay

There are many types of essays, but in general, they are usually short compositions in which the writer expresses and discusses an opinion about something. In the persuasive essay the writer tries to persuade (convince) the reader to do something or to agree with the writer's opinion about something. Examples of persuasive writing are easy to find. Advertising is one common example. Through commercial and print ads, companies try to convince the public to buy their products for specific reasons. Much everyday writing is persuasive, too. Letters to the editor, posts from sports fans on team Web sites, even handwritten notes urging a friend to listen to a new CD—all are examples of persuasive writing.

The Tools of Persuasion

The writer of the persuasive essay uses various tools to persuade the reader. Here are some of them:

Facts and Statistics. A fact is a statement that no one, typically, would disagree with. It can be verified by information in reputable resources, such as encyclopedias, almanacs, government Web sites, or reference books about the topic of the fact.

Examples of Facts and Statistics

Valentine's Day is celebrated on February 14.

Paris is the capital of France.

The average American uses five hundred gallons of gasoline each year.

According to a June 2008 *Los Angeles Times*/Bloomberg Poll, 67 percent of Americans believe the Iraq War was not worth fighting.

It is important to note that facts and statistics can be *misstated* (written down or quoted incorrectly), *misinterpreted* (not understood correctly by the user), or *misused* (not used fairly). But, if a writer uses facts and statistics properly, they can add authority to the writer's essay.

Opinions. An opinion is what a person thinks about something. It can be contested or argued with. However, opinions of people who are experts on the topic or who have personal experience are often very convincing. Many persuasive essays are written to convince the reader that the writer's opinion is worth believing and acting on.

Testimonials. A testimonial is a statement given by a person who is thought to be an expert or who has another trait people admire, such as being a celebrity. Television commercials frequently use testimonials to convince watchers to buy the products they are advertising.

Examples and Anecdotes. An example is something that is representative of a group or type ("linguini" is an example of the group "pasta"). Examples are used to help define, describe, or illustrate something to make it more understandable. Anecdotes are extended examples. They are little stories with a beginning, middle, and end. They can be used just like examples to explain something or to show something about a topic.

Appeals to Reason. One way to convince readers that an opinion or action is right is to appeal to reason or logic. This often involves the idea that if some ideas are true, another must also be true. Here is an example of one type of appeal to reason:

- Turtle Homes Rescue is an organization that rescues many turtles every year.
- Turtle Homes Rescue needs money to keep operating. Therefore, if you love animals, you should contribute money to Turtle Homes Rescue.

Appeals to Emotion. Another way to persuade readers to believe or do something is to appeal to their emotions—love, fear, pity, loyalty, and anger are some of the emotions to which writers appeal. A writer who wants to persuade the reader that Americans should be drafted into the military might appeal to the reader's sense of loyalty: "Every American must equally share the responsibility of protecting this nation—we cannot let only the bravest and most responsible members of society carry this heavy burden that benefits us all."

Ridicule and Name-Calling. Ridicule and name-calling are not good techniques to use in a persuasive essay. Instead of exploring the strengths of the topic, the writer who uses these relies on making those who oppose the main idea look foolish, evil, or stupid. In most cases, the writer who does this weakens the argument.

Bandwagon. The writer who uses the bandwagon technique uses the idea that "everybody thinks this or is doing this; therefore it is valid." The bandwagon method is not a very authoritative way to convince your reader of your point.

Words and Phrases Common to Persuasive Essays

accordingly	it seems clear that
because	it stands to reason
consequently	it then follows that
clearly	obviously
for this reason	since
this is why	subsequently
indeed	therefore
it is necessary to	thus
it makes sense to	we must

The Government Does Not Belong at Our Dinner Tables

Editor's Notes The first model essay argues that it is not the government's job to reduce obesity. The author explains why she believes that individuals should be allowed to make decisions about what they eat and how they exercise without pressure or involvement from the government. The essay is structured as a five-paragraph essay in which each paragraph contributes a supporting piece of evidence to develop the argument.

The notes in the margin point out key features of the essay and will help you understand how the essay is organized. Also note that all sources are cited using Modern Language Association (MLA) style.* For more information on how to cite your sources, see Appendix C. In addition, consider the following:

■ Refers to thesis and topic sentences

■ Refers to supporting details

1. How does the introduction engage the reader's attention?
2. What persuasive techniques are used in the essay?
3. What purpose do the essay's quotes serve?
4. Does the essay convince you of its point?

Paragraph 1

In 1967, when he was justice minister of Canada, Pierre Trudeau famously said, "There's no place for the state in the bedrooms of the nation." Those famous words have come to represent what most Americans feel about the role of government in their private lives: that the state should not, and cannot, tell them what to think, whom to love, where to work, and more. Yet a movement underway in the United States and other nations has many appealing to the government to take responsibility for making Americans

Look at Exercise 3A on introductions. What type of introduction is this? Does it grab your attention?

---

* Editor's Note: In applying MLA style guidelines in this book, the following simplifications have been made: Parenthetical text citations are confined to direct quotations only; electronic source documentation in the Works Cited list omits date of access, page ranges, and some detailed facts of publication.

This is the essay's thesis statement. It gets to the heart of the author's argument.

thinner and in better shape. While these are noble goals, it is not the government's job to make Americans eat right, exercise, or avoid certain foods.

Paragraph 2

This is the topic sentence of Paragraph 2. It is a subset of the essay's thesis. It tells what specific point this paragraph will be about.

First, it seems as if the obesity "crisis" is not a crisis at all, and certainly not bad enough to warrant government involvement in the problem. Although studies by the Centers for Disease Control and Prevention (CDC) had long warned that almost 400,000 people die each year from obesity and obesity-related causes, skepticism and criticism eventually caused them in 2005 to recheck their work. When they did, they found that obesity-related deaths actually only account for 25,814 deaths—a fraction of the original estimate. In fact, this revisal ranked obesity as No. 7, instead of No. 2, on the nation's list of preventable causes of death. That such a large correction was needed made it exceedingly obvious that the government has exaggerated the problem of obesity. As one analyst puts it, "While government officials insist America is suffering from an epidemic of obesity, it's more like an epidemic of obesity myths" (Berman).

Analyze this quote. What do you think made the author want to select it for inclusion in the essay?

Paragraph 3

This is the topic sentence of Paragraph 3. Without reading the rest of the paragraph, take a guess at what the paragraph will be about.

Not only is obesity much less of a problem than once thought, but designating certain foods as more "dangerous" than others violates the free market principles that this country is founded on. As long as a product is not toxic or imminently dangerous, and as long as its health risks are adequately advertised (as are health warnings on cigarettes), it is free to be sold as per the market's demand for it. In other words, if people want to buy a reasonably safe product, it is not the government's business to tell them they shouldn't or can't. Yet calls for fast food to bear cigarette-style warning levels and for junk food to be banned on school campuses continue to ring out from the anti-obesity crusaders. It is not fair to cripple the sales of products the people clearly want when there is not a demonstrated threat to public health or safety.

The author is expressing her opinion in an attempt to get the reader to agree with her point of view. Did it work? Do you agree with her?

Paragraph 4

Finally, making the government responsible for reducing obesity robs Americans of the freedom guaranteed to them under the Constitution. Being an American means being free to make your own decisions. Ours is a country in which no one can tell you what to wear, listen to, read, or say, so long as you are not doing unreasonable damage to others. This is why even though cigarettes, alcohol, and soda may be bad for a person, it is his or her right to enjoy these products. When we suggest the government should be at the helm of reducing obesity, we turn ourselves into children who need to be babysat by the state. As policy analysts Patrick Basham and John Luik argue, "The obesity crusade presumes a nursery nation comprised of docile infant-citizens too uncertain of their own values to be left to make their own way in a world in which an evil Ronald McDonald lurks under every archway."

This is the topic sentence of Paragraph 4. It explores a different facet of the essay's thesis than the other paragraphs.

What point in Paragraph 4 does this quote support? Note that it was taken from Viewpoint Two. The author selected it because it is well written and from credible experts.

Paragraph 5

Once the government starts telling us what to eat and when to exercise, what will come next? Will our senators remind us to brush our teeth every night before bed? Will the National Guard be dispatched to make sure everyone goes to bed on time and gets a good night's sleep? Americans must be encouraged to make their own decisions and to take responsibility for their actions. The government has no place at American dinner tables, and we must reject all efforts that encourage it to pull up a chair.

Note how the author returns to ideas introduced in Paragraph 1. See Exercise 3A for more on introductions and conclusions.

Works Cited

Basham, Patrick, and John Luik. "Four Big, Fat Myths." *Telegraph* [London] 27 Nov. 2006 < www.telegraph.co.uk/news/main.jhtml?xml = /news/2006/11/26/nfat26.xml&page = 1 > .

Berman, Rick. "Industry Salivates over New Cash Cow." *Atlanta Journal Constitution* 23 Feb. 2005.

Trudeau, Pierre. "Trudeau's Omnibus Bill: Challenging Canadian Taboos." 21 Dec. 1967 < http://archives.cbc.ca/politics/rights_freedoms/topics/538/ > .

Exercise 1A: Create an Outline from an Existing Essay

It often helps to create an outline of the five-paragraph essay before you write it. The outline can help you organize the information, arguments, and evidence you have gathered during your research.

For this exercise, create an outline that could have been used to write *The Government Does Not Belong at Our Dinner Tables*. This "reverse engineering" exercise is meant to help familiarize you with how outlines can help classify and arrange information.

To do this you will need to
1. articulate the essay's thesis
2. pinpoint important pieces of evidence
3. flag quotes that support the essay's ideas, and
4. identify key points that support the argument.

Part of the outline has already been started to give you an idea of the assignment.

Outline

I. Paragraph 1
Write the essay's thesis: It is not the government's job to make Americans eat right, exercise, or avoid certain foods.

II. Paragraph 2
Topic:

  Supporting Detail i.

  Supporting Detail ii. Rich Berman quote that supports the idea that the obesity crisis is not bad enough to warrant government intervention.

III. Paragraph 3
Topic: Designating certain foods as more "dangerous" than others is a violation of free market principles.

Supporting Detail i. Argument that if people want to buy a reasonably safe product, it is not the government's business to tell them they shouldn't or can't.
Supporting Detail ii.

IV. Paragraph 4
Topic:
   Supporting Detail i.

   Supporting Detail ii.

V. Paragraph 5:
Write the essay's conclusion:

Exercise 1B: Create an Outline for Your Own Essay

The model essay you just read expresses a particular point of view about obesity. For this exercise, your assignment is to find supporting ideas, choose specific and concrete details, create an outline, and ultimately write a five-paragraph essay making a different, or even opposing, point about obesity. Your goal is to use persuasive techniques to convince your reader.

Part 1: Write a thesis statement.

The following thesis statement would be appropriate for an opposing essay on why the government should take responsibility for reducing obesity:

> *We have charged our leaders with protecting us from disease outbreaks, terrorism, and other threats to public safety—why not also charge them with protecting us from obesity, which kills thousands every year?*

Or see the sample paper topics suggested in Appendix D for more ideas.

Part II: Brainstorm pieces of supporting evidence.

Using information from some of the viewpoints in the previous section and from the information found in Section Three of this book, write down three arguments or pieces of evidence that support the thesis statement you selected. Then, for each of these three arguments, write down supportive facts, examples, and details that support it. These could be

- statistical information;
- personal memories and anecdotes;
- quotes from experts, peers, or family members;
- observations of people's actions and behaviors;
- specific and concrete details.

Supporting pieces of evidence for the above sample thesis statement are found in this book and include:

- Discussion in Viewpoint Three of the numerous health risks of obesity.
- Suggestion made in Viewpoint Five that the government should have a National Strategy to Combat Obesity, the same way it has national strategies to deal with a pandemic flu outbreak or other national disasters.
- Chart accompanying Viewpoint Five showing that the majority of Americans believe the government should have a role in the fight against obesity.

Part III: Place the information from Part I in outline form.

Part IV: Write the arguments or supporting statements in paragraph form.

By now you have three arguments that support the paragraph's thesis statement, as well as supporting material. Use the outline to write out your three supporting arguments in paragraph form. Make sure each paragraph has a topic sentence that states the paragraph's thesis clearly and broadly. Then, add supporting sentences that express the facts, quotes, details, and examples that support the paragraph's argument. The paragraph may also have a concluding or summary sentence.

Schools Should Help Reduce Child Obesity

Editor's Notes The following model essay argues that schools are responsible for preventing child obesity. Like the first model essay, this essay is structured as a five-paragraph persuasive essay in which each paragraph contributes a supporting piece of evidence to develop the argument. Three distinct ways in which schools could prevent students from becoming overweight or obese are explored.

As you read this essay, take note of its components and how they are organized. (The notes in the margins provide further explanation.)

Paragraph 1

Child obesity has reached crisis proportions in America. Approximately 25 million American children are currently classified as obese or overweight, according to the group Trust for America's Health. In their opinion, "Today's children are likely to be the first generation to live shorter, less healthy lives than their parents" (Levi et al. 3). Since the vast majority of American children attend school, and do so during the years in which they form lifelong dietary and physical habits, schools should be considered the front lines of defense against child obesity.

This is the essay's thesis statement. It tells the reader what will be argued in the following paragraphs.

Paragraph 2

The center of the school's effort against child obesity should be the cafeteria. Consider that students typically eat at least one meal a day at school (sometimes two if they participate in a breakfast program). The typical school year runs 185 days. If the average student eats three meals a day, 365 days a year, and if 185 of those meals come from a school's cafeteria, that makes 17 percent—nearly a fifth—of all the food a student eats in a whole year cafeteria-based. This is an enormous opportunity

Note This is the topic sentence of Paragraph 2. It tells you the paragraph will discuss how school cafeterias can be made healthier.

to get healthy food into America's kids! Therefore, only healthy choices should be available for school lunches and breakfasts. Choices could include fresh salads, lean deli sandwiches, fruit, low-fat milk, low-sugar cereal, vegetables, healthy soups, and similar fare. Not only are these foods delicious, but they are healthy and nutritious. If you want to gain direct access to the American teenager's diet, the path is through the school cafeteria.

> "Therefore" and "Not only" are transitional phrases. They keep the sentences linked together and keep ideas moving.

Paragraph 3

Another way in which America's kids could avoid becoming overweight or obese is by increasing physical education requirements in schools. Unfortunately, as a result of steady budget cuts, gym class and extracurricular sports have been phased out of many educational programs. Many schools do not have the funds or staff to support them. According to experts Jeffrey Levi, Emily Gadola, and Laura M. Segal, "Schools should be encouraged to not only increase the amount of time students spend in physical education classes but ensure that enough time is actually being spent in moderate-to-vigorous physical activity before and after school and between classes" (94). Soccer, basketball, wrestling, football, kickball, gymnastics, track and field, and even speed walking are all enjoyable, easy activities that can be incorporated into any school's campus no matter the space or the season.

> What is the topic sentence of Paragraph 3? Look for a sentence that tells generally what the paragraph's main point is.

> This quote was taken from Viewpoint Five. Learn to copy down quotes (and their citation information) that can support points you plan to make in your paper.

Paragraph 4

Finally, school teams, clubs, and schools themselves should be forbidden from selling candy in fund-raising efforts. No one really likes candy anyway, and overweight students certainly do not need it. Instead of peddling unnecessary, fattening foods to an already overweight student body, fund-raisers should sell items that students actually need, such as school supplies or clothing. Another form of fund-raising that should be banned is vending machines. Though not traditionally thought of as a fund-raiser, such machines raise thousands of dollars for schools when placed near bathrooms, hallways, and

> What is the topic sentence of Paragraph 4? How did you recognize it?

What point in Paragraph 4 does this statistic support?

recreational areas. According to the Center for Science in the Public Interest (CSPI), students take in an additional thirty-four thousand calories from vending-machine soft drinks over the course of their four-year high school career. Furthermore, most machines raise an unimpressive amount for schools, topping out at about eighteen dollars per student per year. With this in mind, vending machines that carry soda, candy, and other junk should be restocked with bottled water, seltzer, and healthy snacks such as dried fruit, unsalted nuts, and low-fat pretzels. Schools should replace this lame method of fund-raising with healthy fund-raisers such as walkathons, bike-athons, and healthy food sales. Alicia Millar and Tim Sullivan of *PTO Today,* who have witnessed the successful implementation of such fund-raising efforts, call them "a nice combination" of fund-raising, health, and community action (qtd. in Johanson and Wootan 11).

Paragraph 5

Note how the author returns to ideas about obesity and lifespan that were introduced in Paragraph 1.

These are just a few ideas for making schools healthier places for America's youth. If they are not instituted, it is likely that the child obesity crisis will continue to worsen. Parents, teachers, and school administrators must take immediate action to transform America's schools from houses of fat into houses of health. Nothing less than the health and longevity of the next generation of children is at stake.

Works Cited

Levi, Jeffrey, Emily Gadola, and Laura M. Segal. "F as in Fat: How Obesity Policies Are Failing in America." Trust for America's Health, Aug. 2007 < http://healthyamericans. org/reports/obesity2007/Obesity2007Report.pdf > .

Johanson, Joy, and Margo G. Wootan. "Sweet Deals: School Fundraising Can Be Profitable and Healthy." Center for Science in the Public Interest, Feb. 2007 < http://cspinet. org/new/pdf/schoolfundraising.pdf > .

Exercise 2A: Create an Outline from an Existing Essay

As you did for the first model essay in this section, create an outline that could have been used to write *Schools Should Help Reduce Child Obesity*. Be sure to identify the essay's thesis statement, its supporting ideas, its descriptive passages, and key pieces of evidence that were used.

Exercise 2B: Identify Persuasive Techniques

Essayists use many techniques to persuade you to agree with their ideas or to do something they want you to do. Some of the most common techniques are described in Preface B of this section, "The Persuasive Essay." These tools are facts and statistics, opinions, testimonials, examples and anecdotes, appeals to reason, appeals to emotion, ridicule and name-calling, and bandwagon. Go back to the preface and review these tools. Remember that most of these tools can be used to enhance your essay, but some of them—particularly ridiculing, name-calling, and bandwagon—can detract from the essay's effectiveness. Nevertheless, you should be able to recognize them in the essays you read.

Some writers use one persuasive tool throughout their whole essay. For example, the essay may be one extended anecdote, or the writer may rely entirely on statistics. But most writers typically use a combination of persuasive tools. Model Essay Two, *Schools Should Help Reduce Child Obesity,* does this.

Problem One
Read Model Essay Two again and see if you can find every persuasive tool used. Put that information in the following table. Part of the table is filled in for you.

Explanatory notes are underneath the table. (Note: You will not fill in every box. No paragraph contains all of the techniques.)

	Paragraph 1 Sentence #	Paragraph 2 Sentence #	Paragraph 3 Sentence #	Paragraph 4 Sentence #	Paragraph 5 Sentence #
Fact					
Statistic	2[a]				
Opinion		8[b]			
Testimonial				10[c]	
Example					
Anecdote					
Appeal to Reason					2[d]
Appeal to Emotion					
Ridicule				9[e]	
Name-Calling					
Bandwagon					

Notes

a. That 25 million American children have been classified as overweight or obese is a statistic.

b. That these foods are delicious is an opinion.

c. This quote is from people who have personally instituted these fund-raisers. Their statement is therefore a testimonial.

d. The author is appealing to the readers' sense of reason. If they want child obesity to be reduced, they need to institute these reforms.

e. When the author calls fund-raising efforts "lame" she is ridiculing them. A more appropriate adjective would have been "unhealthy" or "ineffective."

Now, look at the table you have produced. Which persuasive tools does this essay rely on most heavily? Which are not used at all?

Problem Two

Apply this exercise to the other model essays in this section, and the viewpoints in Section One, when you are finished reading them.

The American Way of Life Is Making People Fat

Editor's Notes The final model essay argues that the American way of life has facilitated obesity. Supported by facts, quotes, statistics, and opinions, it tries to persuade the reader that American eating habits, communities, hobbies, and other pastimes have made it easier for men, women, and children to gain excessive amounts of weight.

This essay differs from the previous model essays in that it is longer than five paragraphs. Sometimes five paragraphs are simply not enough to adequately develop an idea. Extending the length of an essay can allow the reader to explore a topic in more depth or present multiple pieces of evidence that together provide a complete picture of a topic. Longer essays can also help readers discover the complexity of a subject by examining a topic beyond its superficial exterior. Moreover, the ability to write a sustained research or position paper is a valuable skill you will need as you advance academically.

As you read, consider the questions posed in the margins. Continue to identify the thesis statement, supporting details, transitions, and quotations. Examine the introductory and concluding paragraphs to understand how they give shape to the essay. Finally, evaluate the essay's general structure, and assess its overall effectiveness.

Refers to thesis and topic sentences

Refers to supporting details

Paragraph 1

Being overweight and being obese have multiple complex causes. Genetics can play a factor, as can a person's natural metabolism and even economic status. In America, however, being overweight and obese is an increasingly common condition. According to the Weight-control Information Network, as of 2008 two-thirds of all Americans—66 percent—were classified as overweight

What is the essay's thesis statement? How did you recognize it?

81

or obese. That makes the United States the fattest nation in the world. A close look at our culture reveals that the American lifestyle is steering Americans toward a high-calorie, sedentary way of life that promotes obesity.

Paragraph 2

What is the thesis statement of Paragraph 2? Look for something that expresses the main point of this paragraph.

One pastime that has promoted obesity and overweight is the American tendency to eat big. We are the people who invented the double cheeseburger; we are the nation that popularized the buffet. As a culture we eschew small portions and mock fancy food that comes in tiny, artistic servings on large, decorated plates. We think more is automatically better and tastier. As one Londoner stationed in New York observed, "Eating big is as much a part of the American experience as, well, apple pie (with Reddi-wip from an aerosol on top)" (Usborne). Indeed, our super-sized palates and preferences have heralded the popularity of wholesaler shops such as Costco, Sam's Club, and BJ's: originally designed for restauranteurs and small business owners, such buy-in-bulk, large-portion warehouse stores are now frequented mainly by the ever-growing American family.

Paragraph 3

Not only are Americans eating big, but they are doing so in a hurry. In fact, eating quickly or on the go is not only an American habit, but tied in with one of its most cherished pastimes: driving. Increasingly crunched for time, many people grab food to eat as they are driving. In fact, a 2004 PEMCO Insurance poll found that eating is the number one activity drivers do while driving—65 percent of American drivers stated they eat while driving. According to Dr. Gina Scarano-Osika, eating while driving constitutes "unconscious eating," a period of eating during which "your mind is typically blank and you don't know for sure how many minutes went by, never mind how many calories were consumed." A person's ability to determine when they are full, along with their ability to make conscious decisions about what to eat, become

Make a list of everyone quoted in this essay. What types of people have been quoted? What makes them qualified to speak on this topic?

dulled when they eat in this state. As a result, Americans who eat while driving typically eat higher-calorie and fatty foods, and more of them.

Paragraph 4

The automobile has not only become a substitute for the dining room but is also the place where Americans expend few calories as they sit for hours each day behind the wheel. According to a 2005 study by the Texas Transportation Institute, the average American commuter spends about 38 hours—almost a full work week—stuck in their car every year. People who live in or near especially crowded cities sit in their cars even longer. Researchers found that commuters in Los Angeles and its surrounding areas spend approximately 72 hours a year stuck in their cars. This sedentary time spent in cars has worsened over the last few decades. In 1985 Americans spent about 18 hours a year commuting in their cars. Twenty years later that amount of time had more than doubled—as did the waistlines of many Americans who traded time they could have been exercising for time spent in traffic. When one considers that traffic has worsened and commutes have grown longer than they ever have been, it seems no wonder that Americans have become heavier.

What persuasive technique is the author using here? See Preface B in this section for information on persuasive techniques.

Paragraph 5

But even when they are not commuting to work, Americans still tend to drive more and walk less. There is no question that the United States is an automobile-centric society. People tend to hop in their cars to run an errand, rather than walk or ride a bike. One reason for this is the way in which American communities shifted from urban to suburban places throughout the twentieth century. Land in the suburbs tends to be less expensive than in the city, and the extra space attracts families who want their kids to be able to play in a private yard. But living in the suburbs means driving almost everywhere: to work, to school, to shopping, and to entertainment. In addition, some urban

Make a list of all the transitions that appear in the essay and how they keep the ideas flowing.

areas, such as Phoenix, have become sprawling and huge, making walking to work, school, shopping, and entertainment difficult or impossible. When they cannot walk, run, or bike to accomplish daily errands, Americans miss out on yet another exercise opportunity.

Paragraph 6

The high level of modernization enjoyed by Americans further contributes to their low levels of activity and high rates of overweight and obesity. Elevators and escalators are the norm in most buildings and are frequently used by people instead of stairs. Most modern airports, many malls, and even some outdoor areas (such as the Strip in Las Vegas) feature moving sidewalks that passively transport people across easily walkable distances. Furthermore, modern appliances such as dishwashers, washer/dryers, and vacuum cleaners take most of the muscle out of housework. Indeed, previous generations expended hundreds of calories doing chores and errands that now need only the push of a button. Though modern technology has made life infinitely more convenient, it has also cut down on the opportunity to be active during the day. Steven Blair of the Cooper Institute for Aerobics Research in Dallas testified before Congress about this very problem. "How many of you order Christmas presents now over the Internet?" he asks. "Shopping is not your basic aerobic training activity. But it does spend more calories than sitting at your computer shopping over the Internet. . . . We've engineered activity out of daily life" (qtd. in "Dietary Guidelines Advisory Committee Meeting Transcript").

What pieces of this essay are opinions? What parts are facts? Make a list of opinions and facts and see which the author relies on more.

Paragraph 7

A final way in which the American lifestyle has promoted obesity is a result of increasing numbers of women in the workforce. Indeed, more families than ever before have two parents who both work outside the home. According to the opinion research organization Public Agenda, more than 60 percent of married women with young children

What is the topic sentence of Paragraph 7?

work outside the home, and 39 percent work in full-time jobs. While this means more income generated for struggling families, it means less time to prepare wholesome nutritious meals. When both parents work, and no one is at home to prepare meals, the push toward eating out or getting fast food is even stronger. Surely, an equal opportunity for an enlarged waistline was not the kind of progress America's feminists were envisioning when they championed women's rights.

What pieces of evidence are used to show that it is true?

Paragraph 8

Women in the workforce, modern appliances, traffic, and suburban communities are just a few of the features of American life that have contributed to swelling rates of overweight and obesity in this country. If Americans want to seriously tackle the growing obesity crisis, they will need to think long and hard about aspects of their culture that promote it and take rapid action toward change.

After reading the essay, are you convinced of the author's point? If so, what evidence swayed you? If not, why not?

Works Cited

"Dietary Guidelines Advisory Committee Meeting Transcript." Dietary Guidelines Advisory Committee. 16–18 Jun. 1999 < www.health.gov/dietaryguidelines/dgac/dg_0616.htm >

Scarano-Osika, Gina. "Unconscious Eating." Friendly Mirrors.com 2008 < www.friendlymirrors.com/unconscious_eating.php >

Usborne, David. "Our Man in New York: Healthy Eating in America—Fat Chance." *Independent* [London] 16 Mar. 2004.

Exercise 3A: Examining Introductions and Conclusions

Every essay features introductory and concluding paragraphs that are used to frame the main ideas being presented. Along with presenting the essay's thesis statement, well-written introductions should grab the attention of the reader and make clear why the topic being explored is important. The conclusion reiterates the essay's thesis and is also the last chance for the writer to make an impression on the reader. Strong introductions and conclusions can greatly enhance an essay's effect on an audience.

The Introduction

There are several techniques that can be used to craft an introductory paragraph. An essay can start with:

- an anecdote: a brief story that illustrates a point relevant to the topic;
- startling information: facts or statistics that elucidate the point of the essay;
- setting up and knocking down a position: a position or claim believed by proponents of one side of a controversy, followed by statements that challenge that claim;
- historical perspective: an example of the way things used to be that leads into a discussion of how or why things work differently now;
- summary information: general introductory information about the topic that feeds into the essay's thesis statement.

1. Reread the introductory paragraphs of the model essays and of the viewpoints in Section One. Identify which of the techniques described above are used in the example essays. How do they grab the attention of the reader? Are thesis statements clearly presented?
2. Write an introduction for the essay you have outlined and partially written in Exercise 1B using one of the techniques described above.

The Conclusion

The conclusion brings the essay to a close by summarizing or returning to its main ideas. Good conclusions, however, go beyond simply repeating these ideas. Strong conclusions explore a topic's broader implications and reiterate why it is important to consider. They may frame the essay by returning to an anecdote featured in the opening paragraph. Or they may close with a quotation or refer to an event in the essay. In opinionated essays, the conclusion can reiterate which side the essay is taking or ask the reader to reconsider a previously held position on the subject.

3. Reread the concluding paragraphs of the model essays and of the viewpoints in Section One. Which were most effective in driving their arguments home to the reader? What sorts of techniques did they use to do this? Did they appeal emotionally to the reader or bookend an idea or event referenced elsewhere in the essay?

4. Write a conclusion for the essay you have outlined and partially written in Exercise 1B using one of the techniques described above.

Exercise 3B: Using Quotations to Enliven Your Essay

No essay is complete without quotations. Get in the habit of using quotes to support at least some of the ideas in your essays. Quotes do not need to appear in every paragraph, but often enough so that the essay contains voices aside from your own. When you write, use quotations to accomplish the following:

- Provide expert advice that you are not necessarily in the position to know about.
- Cite lively or passionate passages.
- Include a particularly well-written point that gets to the heart of the matter.
- Supply statistics or facts that have been derived from someone's research.

- Deliver anecdotes that illustrate the point you are trying to make.
- Express first-person testimony.

Problem One:
Reread the essays presented in all sections of this book, and find at least one example of each of the above quotation types.

There are a couple of important things to remember when using quotations:

- Note your sources' qualifications and biases. This way your reader can identify the person you have quoted and can put their words in a context.
- Put any quoted material within proper quotation marks. Failing to attribute quotes to their authors constitutes plagiarism, which is when an author takes someone else's words or ideas and presents them as his or her own. Plagiarism is a very serious infraction and must be avoided at all costs.

Write Your Own Persuasive Five-Paragraph Essay

Using the information from this book, write your own five-paragraph persuasive essay that deals with obesity. You can use the resources in this book for information about issues relating to this topic and how to structure this type of essay.

The following steps are suggestions on how to get started.

Step One: Choose your topic.
The first step is to decide what topic to write your persuasive essay on. Is there any subject that particularly fascinates you about obesity? Is there an issue you strongly support or feel strongly against? Is there a topic you feel personally connected to or one that you would like to learn more about? Ask yourself such questions before selecting your essay topic. Refer to Appendix D: Sample Essay Topics if you need help selecting a topic.

Step Two: Write down questions and answers about the topic.
Before you begin writing, you will need to think carefully about what ideas your essay will contain. This is a process known as *brainstorming*. Brainstorming involves asking yourself questions and coming up with ideas to discuss in your essay. Possible questions that will help you with the brainstorming process include:

- Why is this topic important?
- Why should people be interested in this topic?
- How can I make this essay interesting to the reader?
- What question am I going to address in this paragraph or essay?
- What facts, ideas, or quotes can I use to support the answer to my question?

Questions especially for persuasive essays include:
- Is there something I want to convince my reader of?
- Is there a topic I want to advocate in favor of, or rally against?

- Is there enough evidence to support my opinion?
- Do I want to make a call to action—motivate my readers to do something about a particular problem or event?

Step Three: Gather facts, ideas, and anecdotes related to your topic.

This book contains several places to find information about many aspects of obesity, including the viewpoints and the appendices. In addition, you may want to research the books, articles, and Web sites listed in Section Three, or do additional research in your local library. You can also conduct interviews if you know someone who has a compelling story that would fit well in your essay.

Step Four: Develop a workable thesis statement.

Use what you have written down in steps two and three to help you articulate the main point or argument you want to make in your essay. It should be expressed in a clear sentence and make an arguable or supportable point.

Example:

People, not corporations, make themselves fat.
This could be the thesis statement of a persuasive essay that argues that fast food corporations are not responsible for obesity.

Step Five: Write an outline or diagram.

1. Write the thesis statement at the top of the outline.
2. Write roman numerals I, II, and III on the left side of the page. Under each numeral write the letters A, B, and C.
3. Next to each roman numeral, write down the best ideas you came up with in step three. These should all directly relate to and support the thesis statement.
4. Next to each letter, write down information that supports that particular idea.

Step Six: Write the three supporting paragraphs.

Use your outline to write the three supporting paragraphs. Write down the main idea of each paragraph in sentence form. Do the same thing for the supporting points of information. Each sentence should support the paragraph of the topic. Be sure you have relevant and interesting details, facts, and quotes. Use transitions when you move from idea to idea to keep the text fluid and smooth. Sometimes, although not always, paragraphs can include a concluding or summary sentence that restates the paragraph's argument.

Step Seven: Write the introduction and conclusion.
See Exercise 3A for information on writing introductions and conclusions.

Step Eight: Read and rewrite.
As you read, check your essay for the following:

- ✔ Does the essay maintain a consistent tone?
- ✔ Do all paragraphs reinforce your general thesis?
- ✔ Do all paragraphs flow from one to the other? Do you need to add transition words or phrases?
- ✔ Have you quoted from reliable, authoritative, and interesting sources?
- ✔ Is there a sense of progression throughout the essay?
- ✔ Does the essay get bogged down in too much detail or irrelevant material?
- ✔ Does your introduction grab the reader's attention?
- ✔ Does your conclusion reflect on any previously discussed material or give the essay a sense of closure?
- ✔ Are there any spelling or grammatical errors?

Section Three: Supporting Research Material

Facts About Obesity

Obesity in America

According to the Obesity Action Coalition (OAC):

- One in three American adults is obese.
- Approximately 93 million Americans are obese.

According to the Centers for Disease Control and Prevention (CDC):

- Though it was once thought that 300,000 deaths per year could be linked to overweight and obesity-related causes, in 2005 this number was revised to just over 25,000 deaths per year.
- On average, American adults eat a diet that is made up of approximately 34 percent fat.
- American adults eat a diet that is made up of 12 percent saturated fats.
- Morbid obesity is characterized by being more than one hundred pounds overweight or by having a BMI of 40 or higher.
- Twenty-five percent of morbidly obese people are treated for six or more comorbid conditions.
- An adult with a body mass index of less than 18.5 is considered underweight.
- An adult with a BMI between 18.5 and 24.9 is considered of normal weight.
- An adult with a BMI between 25 and 29.9 is considered overweight.
- An adult with a BMI of 30 or higher is considered obese.
- Women with the same BMI as men often have more body fat.

According to the Center for Consumer Freedom:

- Deaths from being overweight and obese are exaggerated.

- A study published in the *Journal of the American Medical Association* found no link between a BMI of 25 to 29.9 and an increase in the risk of death.
- Being overweight but fit may actually be healthier than dieting to achieve a normal BMI that indicates a normal weight. As a result, being overweight may actually save 86,094 lives each year.
- Most deaths attributed to obesity are of individuals with a BMI of 35 and above.
- Only 8 percent of the population has a BMI in this range.
- When the federal government redefined "overweight" in 2004, more than 35 million Americans who were of normal weight were immediately reclassified as overweight. This redefinition added 22 percent to the number of overweight or obese Americans.
- According to the BMI calculator, 97 percent of NFL football players are overweight, and 50 percent are obese.
- Bruce Willis, Harrison Ford, and George Clooney are all considered overweight with a BMI of 29.4.

According to Obesity in America.org, a Web site run by the Endocrine Society and the Hormone Foundation:
- The annual cost of overweight and obesity in the U.S. is $122.9 billion.
- This accounts for $64.1 billion in direct costs and $58.8 billion in indirect costs related to the obesity epidemic.
- In total, these costs are comparable to the economic costs of cigarette smoking.

Obesity Around the World
According to the World Health Organization (WHO):
- One billion adults worldwide are overweight.
- Approximately 300 million of those adults are classified as obese.
- Approximately 22 million children, worldwide, under age five are overweight.

- Between 2 and 7 percent of total health-care costs worldwide can be attributed to obesity.
- Current obesity levels range from below 5 percent in China, Japan, and certain African nations, to over 75 percent in urban Samoa.

Children and Obesity

According to the American Academy of Child and Adolescent Psychiatry:

- Between 16 and 33 percent of children are obese.
- Obesity-related health costs are estimated at nearly $100 billion annually.
- Overweight children are likely to become overweight adults.
- Children who are obese between the ages of ten and thirteen have an 80 percent chance of becoming obese adults.

According to the CDC:

- National Health and Nutrition Examination Statistics (NHANES) show an increase in the number of overweight and obese children in all age groups.
- Approximately 13.9 percent of children aged two to five are overweight.
- Approximately 18.8 percent of children aged six to eleven are overweight.
- Approximately 17.4 percent of children aged twelve to nineteen are overweight.
- Approximately 19.1 percent of non-Hispanic, Caucasian boys between twelve and nineteen are overweight.
- An estimated 18.5 percent of non-Hispanic, African American boys between twelve and nineteen are overweight.
- Approximately 18.3 percent of Mexican American boys between twelve and nineteen are overweight.
- Non-Hispanic Caucasian and African American adolescent boys showed larger weight gain than Mexican American adolescent boys.

- Approximately 25.4 percent of non-Hispanic, African American girls between twelve and nineteen are overweight.
- An estimated 15.4 percent of non-Hispanic Caucasian girls between twelve and nineteen are overweight.
- Approximately 14.1 percent of Mexican American girls between twelve and nineteen are overweight.
- Non-Hispanic, African American adolescent girls showed larger weight gain than non-Hispanic Caucasian and Mexican American adolescent girls.

According to the WHO:
- Type 2 diabetes now affects obese children before puberty begins.
- The number of overweight children has doubled since 1980.
- The number of overweight teens has tripled since 1980.
- The number of obese children six to eleven years old has more than doubled since 1960.

According to the Center for Science in the Public Interest (CSPI), the average number of soft drinks high school students buy from school vending machines provides an extra thirty-four thousand calories over four years.

According to Obesity in America.org, approximately 25 to 30 percent of adult obesity cases begin with childhood obesity.

American Opinions About Obesity

A 2006 poll by Research America and the Endocrine Society found that:
- 52 percent think obesity is a public health issue that society should help solve.
- 46 percent say it is a private issue that people should deal with on their own.

- 27 percent of Americans named obesity as the top health issue for kids.

When asked whose responsibility it is to address obesity (respondents were allowed to pick multiple answers):
- 98 percent of respondents said parents.
- 96 percent said individuals.
- 87 percent said schools.
- 84 percent said health-care providers.
- 81 percent said the food industry.
- 67 percent said the government.

Finding and Using Sources of Information

No matter what type of essay you are writing, it is necessary to find information to support your point of view. You can use sources such as books, magazine articles, newspaper articles, and online articles.

Using Books and Articles

You can find books and articles in a library by using the library's computer or cataloging system. If you are not sure how to use these resources, ask a librarian to help you. You can also use a computer to find many magazine articles and other articles written specifically for the Internet.

You are likely to find a lot more information than you can possibly use in your essay, so your first task is to narrow it down to what is likely to be most usable. Look at book and article titles. Look at book chapter titles, and examine the book's index to see if it contains information on the specific topic you want to write about. (For example, if you want to write about fast food and you find a book about obesity, check the chapter titles and index to be sure it contains information about fast food specifically before you bother to check out the book.)

For a five-paragraph essay, you do not need a great deal of supporting information, so quickly try to narrow down your materials to a few good books and magazine or Internet articles. You do not need dozens. You might even find that one or two good books or articles contain all the information you need.

You probably do not have time to read an entire book, so find the chapters or sections that relate to your topic, and skim these. When you find useful information, copy it onto a note card or notebook. You should look for supporting facts, statistics, quotations, and examples.

Using the Internet

When you select your supporting information, it is important that you evaluate its source. This is especially important with information you find on the Internet. Because nearly anyone can put information on the Internet, there is as much bad information as good information. Before using Internet Information—or any information—try to determine if the source seems to be reliable. Ask yourself the following questions:

- Is the author or Internet site sponsored by a legitimate organization?
- Is it from a government source?
- Does the author have any special knowledge or training relating to the topic you are looking up?
- Does the article give any indication of where its information comes from?

Using Your Supporting Information

When you use supporting information from a book, article, interview or other source, there are three important things to remember:

1. *Make it clear whether you are using a direct quotation or a paraphrase.* If you copy information directly from your source, you are quoting it. You must put quotation marks around the information and tell where the information comes from. If you put the information in your own words, you are paraphrasing it.

   Here is an example of a using a quotation:
   There appears to be little evidence linking obesity with compromised health. According to Professor Paul Campos, "Save for exceptions involving truly extreme cases, the medical literature simply does not support the claim that higher than average weight is a significant independent health risk." (20)

Here is an example of a brief paraphrase of the same passage:

There appears to be little evidence linking obesity with compromised health. Professor Paul Campos is just one expert who has read numerous studies, papers, and articles that all seem to indicate the health risks of obesity do not pan out. Being overweight or obese, in other words, does not by itself seem to constitute any particular health risk.

2. *Use the information fairly.* Be careful to use supporting information in the way the author intended it. For example, it is unfair to quote an author as saying, "School cafeterias should sell junk food," when he or she intended to say, "School cafeterias should sell junk food about as much as school infirmaries should sell drugs." This is called taking information out of context. This is using supporting evidence unfairly.

3. *Give credit where credit is due.* Giving credit is known as citing. You must use citations when you use someone else's information, but not every piece of supporting information needs a citation.

   - If the supporting information is general knowledge—that is, it can be found in many sources—you do not have to cite your source.
   - If you directly quote a source, you must cite it.
   - If you paraphrase information from a specific source, you must cite it.

If you do not use citations where you should, you are *plagiarizing*—or stealing—someone else's work.

Citing Your Sources

There are a number of ways to cite your sources. Your teacher will probably want you to do it in one of three ways:

- Informal: As in the example in number 1 above, tell where you got the information as you present it in the text of your essay.
- Informal list: At the end of your essay, place an unnumbered list of all the sources you used. This tells the reader where, in general, your information came from.
- Formal: Use numbered footnotes or endnotes. Footnotes or endnotes are generally placed at the end of an article or essay, although they may be placed elsewhere depending on your teacher's requirements.

Works Cited

Campos, Paul. "Why Our Fears About Fat Are Misplaced." *New Scientist* 1 May 2004: 20–22.

Using MLA Style to Create a Works Cited List

You will probably need to create a list of works cited for your paper. These include materials that you quoted from, relied heavily on, or consulted to write your paper. There are several different ways to structure these references. The following examples are based on Modern Language Association (MLA) style, one of the major citation styles used by writers.

Book Entries

For most book entries you will need the author's name, the book's title, where it was published, what company published it, and the year it was published. This information is usually found on the inside of the book. Variations on book entries include the following:

A book by a single author:
> Simon, Jonathan. *Governing Through Crime: How the War on Crime Transformed American Democracy and Created a Culture of Fear.* New York: Oxford University Press, 2007.

Two or more books by the same author:
> Mernissi, Fatima. *Beyond the Veil.* San Francisco: Saqi Books, 2003.
> ———. *Fear of the Modern World.* New York: Basic Books, 2002.

A book by two or more authors:
> Esposito, John L., and Dalia Mogahed. *Who Speaks for Islam? What a Billion Muslims Really Think.* Washington, DC: Gallup Press, 2008.

A book with an editor:
>Friedman, Lauri S., ed. *Writing the Critical Essay: Democracy.* Farmington Hills, MI: Greenhaven, 2008.

Periodical and Newspaper Entries

Entries for sources found in periodicals and newspapers are cited a bit differently than books. For one, these sources usually have a title and a publication name. They also may have specific dates and page numbers. Unlike book entries, you do not need to list where newspapers or periodicals are published or what company publishes them.

An article from a periodical:
>Bauer, Henry H. "The Mystery of HIV/AIDS." *Quadrant* Jul.–Aug. 2006: 61–164.

An unsigned article from a periodical:
>"The Chinese Disease? The Rapid Spread of Syphilis in China." *Global Agenda* 14 Jan. 2007.

An article from a newspaper:
>Bradsher, Keith. "A New, Global Oil Quandary: Costly Fuel Means Costly Calories." *New York Times* 19 Jan. 2008: A2.

Internet Sources

To document a source you found online, try to provide as much information on it as possible, including the author's name, the title of the document, date of publication or of last revision, the URL, and your date of access.

A Web source:
>Butts, Jeffrey. "Too Many Youths Facing Adult Justice." Urban Institute. 25 Aug. 2004. 7 May 2008 < http://www.urban.org/publications/900728.html > .

Your teacher will tell you exactly how information should be cited in your essay. Generally, the very least information needed is the original author's name and the name of the article or other publication.

Be sure you know exactly what information your teacher requires before you start looking for your supporting information so that you know what information to include with your notes.

Sample Essay Topics

Obesity Is a National Crisis

Obesity Is Not a National Crisis

Obesity in Children Is a Serious Problem

Obesity in Children Is Not a Serious Problem

Obesity Is a Serious Problem in Poor and Minority Communities

Being Obese Has Serious Health Risks

The Health Risks of Obesity Are Exaggerated

Overeating and Lack of Exercise Cause Obesity

Overeating and Lack of Exercise Do Not Necessarily Cause Obesity

Junk Food Causes Obesity

Junk Food Does Not Cause Obesity

Fast Food Makes People Obese

Fast Food Does Not Make People Obese

Poor Genetics Cause Obesity

Video Games Contribute to Obesity

The American Lifestyle Causes Obesity

Obesity Is a Disease

Obesity Is Not a Disease

Poor Diet Causes Obesity

Hunger Contributes to Obesity

Gastric Bypass Surgery Can Help Reduce Obesity

Gastric Bypass Surgery May Not Help People Lose Weight

Weight-Loss Drugs Can Help Reduce Obesity

Weight-Loss Drugs Should Not Be Used to Reduce Obesity

Fast Food Restaurants Should Be Required to Fight Obesity

Fast Food Restaurants Should Not Be Required to Fight Obesity

The Government Is Responsible for Combating Obesity

The Government Is Not Responsible for Combating Obesity

Food Manufacturers Are Responsible for Combating Obesity

Food Manufacturers Are Not Responsible for Combating Obesity

Individuals Should Be Held Responsible for Fighting Obesity

Schools are Responsible for Reducing Child Obesity

Parents Are Responsible for Fighting Child Obesity

Organizations to Contact

American Diabetes Association (ADA)

1701 N. Beauregard St., Alexandria, VA 22311
(800) 342-2383 • e-mail: askada@diabetes.org
Web site: www.diabetes.org

The American Diabetes Association, a not-for-profit health organization, works to prevent and cure diabetes, an obesity-related disease. The ADA works to educate people about overweight and obesity because approximately 90 percent of Americans newly diagnosed with type 2 diabetes are overweight or obese. As a part of its program, the ADA provides many tip sheets on overweight and obesity on its Web site, including *Losing Weight: What Does It Take? Be Active: But How?* and *Food and Portion Size.*

American Heart Association (AHA)

7272 Greenville Ave., Dallas, TX 75231 • (800) 242-8721
Web site: www.americanheart.org

The mission of the American Heart Association is to reduce disability and death from cardiovascular diseases and stroke. This voluntary health organization has published a scientific position paper on overweight and obesity because obesity is a major risk factor for coronary heart disease. In addition, the AHA has related scientific position papers and articles on its Web site, including *Obesity and Cardiovascular Disease, Overweight in Children and Adolescents,* and *Clinical Implications of Obesity with Specific Focus on Cardiovascular Disease.*

American Obesity Association (AOA)

1250 Twenty-four St. NW, Ste. 300, Washington, DC 20037
(202) 776-7711 • Web site: www.obesity.org

The American Obesity Association was founded to combat obesity and its health effects. It accomplishes this mission by educating the public about obesity and its association with illness and by promoting obesity research. It also helps protect consumers from diet frauds and scams.

American Society of Bariatric Physicians (ASBP)

2821 S. Parker Rd. Aurora, CO 80014 • (303) 770-2526 fax: (303) 779-4834 • e-mail: info@asb.org
Web site: www.asbp.org

Bariatrics is the medical treatment of obesity and related conditions. The purpose of the American Society of Bariatric Physicians is to support member physicians who treat overweight and obese patients. ASBP provides information on recent developments in the field of obesity to its members and supports public policies to prevent overweight and obesity. The ASBP also provides information on obesity and weight loss to the public.

Centers for Disease Control and Prevention (CDC) Division of Nutrition and Physical Activity (DNPA)

4770 Buford Hwy. NE, MS/K-24, Atlanta, GA 30341-3717 (770) 488-5820 • e-mail: cdcinfo@cdc.gov
Web site: www.cdc.gov/nccdphp/dnpa

The CDC is part of the Department of Health and Human Services (DHHS). Its Division of Nutrition and Physical Activity has three focus areas: nutrition, physical activity, and overweight and obesity. The DNPA addresses the role of nutrition and physical activity in improving the public's health. DNPA activities include health promotion, research, training, and education. The DNPA maintains an overweight and obesity Web page, on which it provides research-based information for consumers.

Food Research and Action Center (FRAC)

1875 Connecticut Ave. NW, Ste. 540 • Washington, DC 20009 (202) 986-2200 • Web site: www.frac.org/index.html

The Food Research and Action Center is the leading national nonprofit organization working to improve public policies and public-private partnerships to eradicate hunger and undernutrition in the United States. FRAC has published several papers about the link between hunger and obesity and works with hundreds of national, state, and local nonprofit organizations, public agencies, and corporations to address this and other food-related problems plaguing Americans.

International Association for the Study of Obesity (IASO)

231 N. Gower St., London NW1 2NR, United Kingdom
+ 44 (0) 20 7691 1900 • e-mail: enquiries@iaso.org
Web sites: www.iaso.org and www.iotf.org

The International Association for the Study of Obesity is a nongovernmental organization with forty-nine member associations representing fifty-three countries. The mission of the IASO is to improve global health by promoting the understanding of obesity and weight-related diseases through scientific research and discussion. The IASO works with the World Health Organization and other global nongovernmental organizations toward this goal.

North American Association for the Study of Obesity (NAASO)

8630 Fenton St., Ste. 918, Silver Spring, MD 20910
(301) 563-6526 • Web site: www.naaso.org

The North American Association for the Study of Obesity encourages research into the causes and treatment of obesity. This scientific society informs the medical community and the public of advances in these areas. The mission of NAASO also includes education and advocacy to help improve the lives of those who are obese.

Obesity Action Coalition (OAC)

4511 N. Himes Ave., Ste. 250, Tampa, FL 33614
(800) 717-3117 • e-mail: info@obesityaction.org
Web site: www.obesityaction.org

The Obesity Action Coalition is a not-for-profit organization that educates not only obesity patients but also their family members and the public. It provides links to resources and obesity support groups throughout the United States. The OAC works against the negative stigma of obesity and is an advocate for safe and effective obesity treatment.

The Obesity Awareness and Solutions Trust (TOAST)

The Latton Bush Centre, Southern Way, Harlow, Essex, UK CM18 7BL • + 44 (0) 12 7986 6010 • e-mail: enquiries@ toast-uk.org.uk • Web site: www.toast-uk.org.uk

This British organization promotes the idea that obesity is a complex problem with no single solution. It says that the treatment and prevention of obesity must go beyond the medical model of diet, exercise, and medication.

The Obesity Society

8630 Fenton St., Ste. 814 • Silver Spring, MD 20910 (301) 563-6526 • Web site: www.obesity.org

The Obesity Society is the leading scientific society dedicated to the study of obesity. Since 1982 its members have been committed to encouraging research on the causes and treatment of obesity and to keeping the medical community and public informed of new advances. The society publishes the journal *Obesity*, which publishes important peer-reviewed research and cutting-edge reviews, commentaries, and public health and medical developments.

Overeaters Anonymous (OA)

World Service Office, PO Box 44020, Rio Rancho, NM 87174-4020 • (505) 891-26642 • e-mail: info@oa.org Web site: www.oa.org

Overeaters Anonymous is an organization open to individuals who wish to, or who are, recovering from compulsive overeating. Individuals share their experiences and support each other to stop eating compulsively. OA provides a twelve-step program, modeled after the twelve-step program of Alcoholics Anonymous, to help members control their food addictions. Members can attend face-to-face meetings in their own localities and can communicate with members worldwide via the Internet.

Shape Up America!
e-mail: info@shapeup.org • Web site: www.shapeup.org

Shape Up America! is a not-for-profit organization founded by former U.S. surgeon general C. Everett Koop. Its mission is to educate the public on how to achieve and maintain a healthy weight. Shape Up America! focuses on behavior change, encouraging increased physical activity and healthy eating.

Take Off Pounds Sensibly (TOPS)
e-mail: topsinteractive@tops.org • Web site: www.tops.org

TOPS is an international not-for-profit weight-loss support group. There are ten thousand chapters worldwide. The mission of TOPS is to support members' efforts to lose weight. The organization uses experts in the field of medical research, nutrition, fitness, and psychology to support its volunteer chapter leaders.

Weight-control Information Network (WIN)
1 WIN Way, Bethesda, MD 20892-3665 • e-mail: win@ info.niddk.nih.gov • Web site: http://win.niddk.nih.gov

WIN is an information service of the National Institute of Diabetes and Digestive and Kidney Diseases (NIDDK). It provides science-based and up-to-date information on weight control, obesity, physical activity, and related nutritional issues.

Bibliography

Books

Gard, Michael, and Jan Wright, *The Obesity Epidemic: Science, Morality, and Ideology*. New York: Taylor and Francis, 2005.

Institute of Medicine, *The Richard and Hinda Rosenthal Lectures 2004: Perspectives on the Prevention of Childhood Obesity in Children and Youth*. Washington, DC: National Academies Press, 2006.

Kaufman, Francine R., *Diabesity: What You Need to Know If Anyone You Care About Suffers from Weight Problems, Pre-Diabetes, or Diabetes*. New York: Bantam, 2006.

McGinnis, J. Michael, et al., eds., *Food Marketing to Children and Youth: Threat or Opportunity?* Washington, DC: National Academies Press, 2006.

Meana, Marta, and Lindsey Ricciardi, *Obesity Surgery: Stories of Altered Lives*. Reno: University of Nevada Press, 2008.

Oliver, J. Eric, *Fat Politics: The Real Story Behind America's Obesity Epidemic*. New York: Oxford University Press, 2005.

Stroebe, Wolfgang, *Dieting, Overweight, and Obesity: Self-Regulation in a Food-Rich Environment*. American Psychological Association, 2008.

Periodicals

Barone, Jennifer, "Whodunnit: TV or Fast Food or Genes? When It Comes to Obesity No One Explanation Tells the Whole Story," *Discover*, June 6, 2008. http://discover magazine.com/2008/jul/03-whodunnit-tv-or-fast-food-or-genes.

Basham, Patrick, and John Luik, "Contestable Conclusions: The Link Between Food, Fat, and Cancer Does Not

Follow from the Available Evidence," *National Review*, November 26, 2007. http://article.nationalreview.com /?q = ZDM3MTg2MmQyOGJmODU0MGFjZTc3Nzk4Z jg3M2ZiNmU = &w = MA.

Campos, Paul, "Why Our Fears About Fat Are Misplaced: The War on Obesity Is Based Not on Sound Science but on Medical Self-Interest and Cultural Hysteria," *New Scientist*, May 1, 2004.

Center for Consumer Freedom, "An Epidemic of Obesity Myths," June 2, 2004. www.consumerfreedom.com/ news_detail.cfm/headline/2535.

Center on Hunger and Poverty and the Food Research and Action Center (FRAC), "The Paradox of Hunger and Obesity," July 17, 2003. www.centeronhunger.org/pdf/ hungerandobesity.pdf.

Chapman, Steve, "Force-Fed the Facts: Will Mandatory Calorie Counts Save Us from Ourselves?" *Reason*, June 23, 2008. www.reason.com/news/show/127126. html.

County of Los Angeles Department of Health Services, "Food Insecurity," March 2004. http://lapublichealth. org/wwwfiles/ph/hae/ha/lahealthfoodinsec_0304. pdf.

Gibbs, W. Wayt, "Obesity: An Overblown Epidemic?" *Scientific American*, May 2005. www.sciam.com/article. cfm?chanID = sa006&colID = 1&articleID = 000E5065- 2345-128A-9E1583414B7F0000.

Glausiusz, Josie, "Big Boned: How Your Skeleton Can Make You Fat," *Discover*, November 23, 2007. http:// discovermagazine.com/2007/nov/big-boned-how- your-skeleton-can-make-you-fat.

Johnson, Patrick, "Epidemic or Myth?" *Skeptical Inquirer*, May 2005. http://csicop.org/si/2005-09/obesity. html.

Lister, Laine, "Tackling Childhood Obesity," *Food Magazine*, September 2006.

Marks, Jennifer B., "Obesity in America: It's Getting Worse," *Clinical Diabetes*, vol. 22, 2004. http://clinical.diabetesjournals.org/cgi/content/full/22/1/1.

Metcalfe, Rob, "Only Idiots Need Food Labels—and They Don't Want Them: Food Labels Alone Will Do Nothing to Stop the Obesity Crisis—People Just Need to Stop Making Excuses for Not Eating a Balanced Diet," *Grocer*, February 2, 2008.

New Scientist, "Can Taxation Curb Obesity?" August 20, 2006.

Reeves, Richard, "The Naughty Nation: Should the State Force Us to Eat Well, Drink Wisely and Behave Nicely on Public Transport, or Should We Leave People Alone Unless They Are Directly Damaging Others? Politicians of All Parties Seem Quite Unable to Get the Balance Right," *New Statesman*, February 14, 2008.

Saletan, William, "Fat Lies: Obesity, Laxity, and Political Correctness," Slate.com, July 26, 2007. www.slate.com/id/2171214.

Stein, Rob, "Fewer U.S. Deaths Linked to Obesity," *Washington Post*, April 20, 2005.

Sullum, Jacob, "The Thin Man Goes to Washington," *Reason*, January 9, 2008. www.reason.com/news/show/124285.html.

Townsend, Marilyn S., Janet Peerson, Bradley Love, Cheryl Achterberg, and Suzanne P. Murphy, "Food Insecurity Is Positively Related to Overweight in Women," *Journal of Nutrition*, vol. 131, no. 6, 2001.

Web Sites

American Cancer Society (ACS) (www.cancer.org). The American Cancer Society, with thousands of local offices throughout the United States, is a voluntary health organization whose mission is to eliminate cancer as a major health problem. Obesity is associated with many cancers, such as those of the breast, esophagus (food tube), large intestine, and kidney. The ACS provides information on obesity and cancer. Its Web site is the home of free articles such as *Obesity Linked to All Types of Breast Cancer, Obesity Linked to Cancer—Other Chronic Disease Risk,* and *Studies Help Clarify Link Between Obesity and Prostate Cancer.* It also has obesity-related Web pages such as *Take Control of Your Weight.*

Centers for Disease Control and Prevention: Overweight and Obesity (www.cdc.gov/nccdphp/dnpa/obesity/index.htm). The CDC's Web site on overweight and obesity provides excellent authoritative resources, such as information on how to achieve and maintain a healthy weight and dietary guidelines for Americans.

Obesity in America (www.obesityinamerica.org). This site, run by the Endocrine Society and the Hormone Foundation, contains a plethora of information about obesity in America. The maps, fact sheets, and brief articles are excellent for students researching reports on the topic.

Obesity Myths (www.obesitymyths.com). This site, run by the Center for Consumer Freedom, offers thoughtful articles and statistics that debunk the conventional wisdom that obesity is an epidemic plaguing Americans.

World Health Organization: Obesity (www.who.int/topics/obesity/en). The World Health Organization (WHO) is the health agency of the United Nations. Its Web site on obesity has links to news, reports, activities, and events on this topic.

Index